PIERRE FOUIN

KICK THOSE SLEEPING DOGS

A PERSONAL JOURNEY THROUGH THE UNCERTAINTIES OF LIFE

PRESS

Published in 2011

Copyright © Pierre Fouin

The right of François Louis Pierre Fouin to be identified as author of
this book has been asserted under the Copyright, Designs and Patents
Act 1988

A catalogue record for this book is available from
the British Library

ISBN 978-0-9534534-9-8

Design and typesetting by
Leopard magazine www.leopardmag.co.uk

Printed and bound in Scotland by Robertson of Forfar

Published by Leopard Press
Auld Logie, Pitcaple, Inverurie, Aberdeenshire AB51 5EE

Dedication

In loving memory of my late wife
Kaye.
In admiration for her courage and stoicism
in the face of terrifying adversity
in striving to achieve
that second chance.

"THE FACT THAT AN OPINION
HAS BEEN WIDELY HELD
IS NO EVIDENCE WHATEVER
THAT IT IS NOT UTTERLY ABSURD: INDEED, IN
VIEW OF THE SILLINESS
OF THE MAJORITY OF MANKIND,
A WIDESPREAD BELIEF IS MORE LIKELY
TO BE FOOLISH THAN SENSIBLE."

BERTRAND RUSSELL
Philosopher
1872–1970

ACKNOWLEDGEMENTS

My colleague Dr George Shirriffs has scanned the pages and given me the encouragement to go ahead and publish. Google has been my ever present friend while *Leopard* has been my bedrock. The editor Lindy Cheyne has been known to use early morning moonlight to bring some brevity to the ramblings while Ian Hamilton, as ever, has been innovative and enthusiastic to bolster my misgivings about the content. My grateful thanks are due to them for their diligence and friendship.

CONTENTS

INTRODUCTION

> **"**LEARN FROM YESTERDAY,
> LIVE FOR TODAY,
> HOPE FOR TOMORROW.
> THE IMPORTANT THING IS
> NOT TO STOP QUESTIONING**"**
>
> *ALBERT EINSTEIN*
> *Theoretical Physicist*
> *(1879–1955)*

Those who have read my two previous books, *Glen Tanar Exile* and the more recent *Glen Tanar Echoes* will find this latest book has departed considerably from the homely comfort of life on a millionaire's estate. True, there are many references to the past, but mostly in the context of how they have influenced my later life.

The introductory quote from Bertrand Russell, the celebrated British philosopher, has mirrored much of my own way of thinking throughout a long life and in the following pages I set out to weigh up the areas where his remarks may be of greatest significance. This is particularly pertinent to religious belief, but also relates to many other areas of every day living that we all too readily and unthinkingly take for granted.

Why I should feel it necessary to launch out on such a book may puzzle many readers, but in a way it is an extension to a rather unusual upbringing and the attempt to think more deeply and widely from the many areas that troubled or intrigued me from childhood. Some may respond that our existence is far too short to go delving into aspects of living, where it is easier just to go with the flow than to challenge perceived wisdoms. For many of us, the problems of trying to blend the ups and downs of family life, employment and leisure are enough without looking for uncertainties which scarcely affect us.

The world changes in less than a decade for our young, with so much gadgetry and fashion unknown to us in our youth. Change, in my childhood, was at a snail's pace with everyone knowing their place, and if you thought you belonged to the class above you were seen as getting too big for your boots. A woman's place was essentially in the home, looking after the children and being a dutiful wife to her hard-working spouse.

Sex was not exactly a dirty word, but to discuss it openly was not regarded as good manners; sexual freedoms in the unmarried young were constrained, by fear, on the woman's part especially, of an unwanted pregnancy. Also, we obeyed much stricter peer group standards regarding manners, school discipline and even to conducting ourselves properly, so that we didn't upset the local bobby.

Religious belief went unchallenged in my youth, but in the UK today we are inundated with literature on this subject from the erudite Professor Richard Dawkins with *The God Delusion* and *The Selfish Gene*, to books of great complexity by scientists, psychologists and theologians. Now, one of the brightest brains of our generation, Professor Stephen Hawking, has accepted that the laws of physics and not God formed the universe. David Attenborough brings a world of unsuspected intricacy into our living rooms, which should unsettle the most ardent creationist, while fiction in the form of Dan Brown's *The Da Vinci Code* makes one wonder whether his plot could be uncomfortably nearer to the true vision of our churches than we innocents have ever contemplated.

As a Humanist, one of my aims in this book is to consider how we came to accept religions, how we see them at the present time and their possible future. I am so aware of the many benefits of modern Christianity that I am keen to find an accommodation between believers and non-believers to strengthen our failing society. For us in the UK to become essentially a secular state, without considering the possible implications, would be to discard so much that is part of the fabric of our society. I seem to have spent a lifetime trying to come to terms with God and the Church, but now I feel I have resolved my own doubts and at last have answered most of the conundrums.

Individual personalities govern our behaviour and dictate our attitudes and I will examine these in order to attempt to explain not only my own actions, but also of those around me. The medical profession is held in high esteem, but doctors, despite their Hippocratic Oath, are ordinary human beings, so how does an insider view his own profession?

For human societies to operate, evolution decrees that the majority of the populace acts simply as followers, so despite the democratic process, most of us remain at the mercy of our leaders and their henchmen. That many of us simply exist from day to day and week to week, confined by small lives, is sad but almost inevitable.

No area of life intrigues me more than the burgeoning spectre of obesity, and the prospect of shortening the lives of our young, instead of lengthening them as is the experience of our own generation.

One of the greatest failings in our society is discussing problems as if we are all similar. The serious media approaches its readership as if the average citizen is middle class, moderately intelligent and responsible. This is farcical and hypocritical, but is the price we pay for not being seen to upset any group, be they stupid, lazy, selfish or religiously misled. For years I have been both baffled and disappointed by blinkered, hypocritical debate. Political correctness has gone a long way to robbing us of forthright open discussion and now we shelter behind bland arguments. Everyone must be respected for what they are and what they believe in, whether it makes sense or not.

I am aware that much that has been written on subjects such as religion is pitched at a level that many may find too complex to comprehend. Add the constant references to multiple scholars and their works, whom we have mostly never heard of, along with mind-boggling acronyms, such as the GIGO principle – garbage in, garbage out – then reading can become a tiresome, unrewarding exercise. I have therefore attempted to discuss subjects clearly and understandably while keeping intricate ivory tower thinking to the minimum.

The views presented in this book are my own, influenced perhaps by others, but certainly not copied. In certain fields, true experts may consider some of my ideas too simplistic or contorted, but this is my evaluation of my world over four score years. I shall always, however, be prepared to reconsider conclusions in the light of convincing evidence.

The title, *Kick Those Sleeping Dogs*, refers to those areas we are only too happy to leave undisturbed, but which are about to be examined in uncompromising detail.

The subtitle, *A Personal Journey through the Uncertainties of Life* gives an insight into the contents, looking at beliefs, opinions, problems and experiences which have continuously buffeted me along the way.

A Highland Setting

"If you carry your childhood with you, you never grow older"

Tom Stoppard
Playwright

The Great War of 1914–1918 had sapped the strength of our once mighty state economically, but had also destroyed our belief in our infallibility. The Victorian era, a world encompassing an empire of power and prestige, had shrivelled in the mud and carnage of the Western Front. The massive losses in dead and wounded had left scarcely a family untouched, yet in some corners of our land much of this was about to be forgotten.

Thomas Coats had come back from the Western Front in 1918 relatively unscathed from his experience of war. The death of his father within days of the armistice left him inheriting the title Lord Glentanar and, along with his ambitious mother, he was to launch himself into the life of the landed gentry. On into the 1920s the nation was striving to blot out the past, led by an extrovert generation of flappers doing the Charleston. The memory of that era in my parent's eyes, was of the rich and powerful throwing themselves into an orgy of the good life to counteract all the suffering that had gone before.

Born into this background in 1928 in Aberdeenshire I was unaware of the world of strikes and economic hardship. The Wall Street crash of 1929, with financiers throwing themselves off skyscrapers, to the Jarrow marchers of 1936, never touched my comfortable life on a millionaire's estate.

Glen Tanar, situated four-and-a-half miles to the south west of the village of Aboyne on Royal Deeside, had been developed a generation before by Sir William Cunliffe Brooks. A national showpiece, it demonstrated what could be achieved among the hills and valleys of Scotland by those willing to spend endless amounts of money. Brooks died in 1900 and in 1905 the estate passed into the hands of the Coats family of the J&P Coats thread empire of Paisley . Money being no object, the estate gave employment to literally hundreds of people, both directly and indirectly, in providing hospitality, leisure and recreation, not only to the wealthy, but also royalty.

Brought up in this well-regulated atmosphere, I was never at a loss to know where I fitted in; the boundaries being well demarcated and strenuously adhered to. No one around me ever murmured dissatisfaction and in fact from memory not many offered an opinion about anything very much. Our thinking on the whole was done, for my generation of workers, by our leaders and employers and those on the estate were only too happy just to be employed there. We lived among some very fine architecture, beautifully laid out gardens and wander walks. Trees and shrubs from distant lands were on show throughout the estate, while Brooks had left behind a welter of inscribed stones, wells, bridges and buildings.

Yet nothing was brought to our attention as children as being worthy of comment. Everything was taken for granted and not even the Glentanar family bothered to widen our horizons as to what lay all around us.

Glentanar School with its lovely twin oast-house roof was never admired, and we ignored all the adages that surrounded us in the classrooms. Looking back, I can scarcely believe that teachers would not have marvelled at the school. Yet no time was ever taken to talk us through those directive sayings or point to the Queen Victoria Diamond Jubilee fountain outside to make us appreciate our history and good fortune.

Hindsight and a life's experience make it easy to be critical and human memory being so fallible, I could well be doing the previous generation a disservice, but life at that time seemed so simple. For the working class the few pleasures came out of a cigarette packet and for some on a Saturday night out of a Johnnie Walker bottle. Local dances, whist drives and ceilidhs formed the entertainment, while modes of transport varied from two feet to the bicycle, and for the very few an ancient motorcycle or Austin 7. I was a privileged child in that I owned a bicycle from an early age, while my cohorts graduated to bicycles only via the Council supplying them so that you could reach school, if you lived some miles away. Neither of my parents owned a bicycle and I have memories of walking with them the four-and-a-half miles to Aboyne and back on occasions. Later in the 1930s the estate provided its own bus to take employees to Aboyne on a Saturday afternoon to do their shopping, which made life much easier for my parents.

The pinnacle of my father's life was acquiring a brand new Austin 10 in 1937. That no one around him had ever owned a new car was something my father revelled in for the next 35 years; today it would be the equivalent of our owning a 60-foot yacht. This achievement was inevitably to rub off on his offspring, although in my lifetime I have never made the comparable jump in material possessions that he made.

My parents had become accustomed to the sheltered, some would say privileged life in service to the wealthy. Both had travelled widely around the world and although neither would have considered themselves truly cultured, my mother seemed to think of herself as just below the upper ten and certainly not working class. My father was more realistic in recognising his position as a personal servant, but he also was adamant in his right to be his own man. Throughout childhood he reminded me I owed respect, but subservience to no one; his favourite quote of his body belonging to his employer, but his mind to himself alone was a powerful message for the young.

Nevertheless, in the setting of the estate I was accepted, despite my odd name, as no different to anyone else and was treated well by teachers and adults alike. Yet, in retrospect I suppose I was a bit of a misfit – an only child, born to elderly parents with a mother who considered herself culturally above her neighbours. I lived in a home that never welcomed strangers and where no entertaining was ever done. Only relatives came to stay and even my pals rarely crossed our threshold. The rigour of 'a place for everything and everything in its place' was something I respected and has lasted into my own life.

Love may not have been very evident among the three of us and my relationship with my mother consisted of doing what I was told, although not always with good grace. However, I have happy memories of a very secure, caring atmosphere, occasionally upset, as described in an earlier book, by the fractious interplay of parents who appeared to have little in common.

Independence of thought was encouraged in our little family and the sheep-like attitudes of many estate employees infuriated my father. He used to get really upset at election time when the laird more or less told him how he expected him to vote, for that jolly good chap, the Tory candidate. If there was anything more certain of getting the opposite response it was intrusion into my father's personal domain. Yet all around him and into the wider community the workers followed the lead of employers and landowners and dutifully put their crosses in the correct box. This memory has influenced me greatly and the lack of independent thought among many of whom you would expect greater things, has made me incandescent throughout my own career.

My secure existence with a mother always on the doorstep to welcome me home from school came to an abrupt end in 1944 when I set out on my own into the strange life of a city. For three years I spent a generally happy time at Aberdeen Grammar School and quickly learnt to blend in with a middle-class setting, far removed from my rural upbringing. With a mother convinced she was almost upper class, I found little difficulty coming to terms with the atmosphere of the school. This sense of belonging continued into my professional life, where I was always to remember my father's advice of Jack being as good as his master. This coupled to my own trait of having no heroes, only people I appreciate because of their qualities, has stood me in good stead throughout my life.

Continuing from school to a university in the same city was seamless, but unhappily my early student years in medicine failed to inspire me. More interested in the dynamics of life around me than in my text books, I began to wonder if drifting into such a prestigious faculty without much thought had been a little too convenient. Rescued by the enthusiasm of my friends, I gradually prospered and realised that medicine, after all, was quite interesting.

Never fired by the passion of many of my associates, I look back on a medical career with a degree of satisfaction. I have made many friends along the way and hope they feel I have been interested in not only their health, but themselves as people. One of my strengths through all those years has been my ability to feel empathy, which balanced any clinical inadequacies I may have had.

I have always felt an urge to back the under privileged, from those bullied in the playground to the poorest patients, some of whom my colleagues would happily overlook. I am a sucker for lost causes and trying to see how to overturn the decisions of our masters. In many ways I feel I missed my vocation as a lawyer, as the little red book of NHS regulations became my bible, and driving a coach and horses through its poorly thought out regulations gave me a real sense of accomplishment.

My need, late in life, to leave behind three books for posterity is probably the peak of my achievements and tells the intuitive observer all about my character. This book is a culmination of years of pondering many taboo subjects and in stirring up so many sleeping dogs, I recognise I may well generate negative feedback. My views are simple and honest, however, and I need to bend the knee to no-one. I hope they stimulate some discussion about subjects which many prefer to leave unmolested.

Now, 82 years old, I consider myself extremely lucky to retain my physical health. Still being a child at heart is a total bonus. In like-minded company I discard all those years of seniority and revel again in those carefree feelings of my youth and those halcyon years on Glen Tanar.

I am certain there are many influences from my childhood which have led me to seeing life through my very own half-tinted glasses. I invite my readers, as they progress through these pages, to sense whether they share anything in common with me, or whether I still exist in my own little world.

A Christian Childhood

"Give me a child until he is seven and I will give you the man"

– A Jesuit Maxim

I was born in the late 1920s when religious belief and adherence to its demands was still hugely important in British society. My mother, born in1892, had religion instilled into her life in a way that totally convinced her, and having lived into her late nineties she fervently believed she was to be taken up into heaven, and there would find peace and tranquillity in God's presence. Her life in the small market town of Morpeth in Northumberland had centred on the church from infancy, until she left for the big time in London in her early twenties. As a teenager she went to church three or four times on Sundays; not only to her own church but to her friends' places of worship and persuasions other than the Church of England. Her memories of singing in church choirs and the happy comradeship shared in this setting filled my own childhood with a lovely sense of warmth, as she reminisced in the evening glow of the fireside before I climbed into bed, having dutifully said my prayers.

My mother lost her first love in World War I on the Western Front in 1917 and then seemed to take an unquestionably long time in deciding to marry my father in 1926. She had known him from around 1916, so it was pretty certain that this was not love at first sight and even in later life she was to question whether she had taken leave of her senses. My father was 45 years old when he married and if my mother was baffled why she married aged 34, I wondered why my father had bothered to settle down and take on life with an extremely difficult lady when he could have continued his own tranquil way of living.

My mother had always made her Christianity a central component of her life. She had a very simple faith and although an intelligent woman she had been so enveloped by her religion from childhood that the possible fallibility of some Christian teachings was unthinkable. In later life I was often to recall that Jesuit saying – give me a child until he is seven and I will give you the man.

My father, born on 12 May 1881 on the farm of La Plonnais outside Chateaubriant in Brittany in France, was unaware of any religion other than Roman Catholicism until he left home for Paris in his teens. The Fouins were local to this area over countless generations as is well documented, allowing me to trace my ancestry back to the early 1600s. At that time there were two branches of the family – one destined to reach the pinnacles of the Catholic Church with bishops listed; the other branch remained firmly rooted in the soil as farmers for generation after generation, until my father broke the mould.

Whether religion caused this break with the past is uncertain, but I am sure it played a part in my father's dissatisfaction for the way of life he foresaw as the eldest son in a large family. The peasantry were in thrall to the Catholic faith in the form of the local priest. A story often repeated to me in childhood to explain why my father was taking no part in my religious upbringing captured my imagination.

My father was about eight years old the year the harvest failed completely and his parents were trying their best to eke out a living while bringing up six young children. He vividly remembered the evening visit that autumn when the priest dropped in to collect his dues. Lying in bed he heard raised voices in the kitchen below and the sound of his mother weeping. Greatly perturbed, he crept to the head of the stair to hear his father pleading to be excused payment as their cupboard was bare. The priest remained unimpressed and my father recalled the threat of religious damnation if the dues were not paid by the following week.

This event was etched into my father's brain and he was to retell the story well into his old age. He could never come to terms with the poverty he saw in the surrounding villages, overseen by magnificent churches, many endowed with gold adornments and sumptuous decoration. He could also visualise the powerful, well- nourished clergy who ruled their flock with a rod of iron. Even in 1937, on my last visit to France before the war, I remember his village church of great splendour, while young urchins in bare feet milled around outside, exuding much the same aura of poverty seen in photos of pre-war Glasgow east-end children.

Turning his back on the Catholic faith was something he attributed to that night of the failed harvest and he apparently never had one moment's regret up to his death in his 98th year. In those days of almost universal faith among French Catholics, my father's action seems all the more extraordinary. Rather than a disbelief in God, it seemed to be a disenchantment with his minions here on earth. Over the years I never actually heard my father say he didn't believe in God, but he did dismiss the Catholic clergy as nothing more than extortionists of the poor.

I doubt whether my father was aware of such terms as atheist or agnostic. It is only now that I begin to comprehend the enormity of his reaction in an age when very few questioned the authenticity of religion, and then only those of a superior, thoughtful intellect. I now very much regret that I did not take a greater interest in uncovering what my father did believe in, as throughout my life I never remember him discussing a belief or a faith.

I was baptised in the Episcopal Chapel of St Lesmo – the private family church of Lord Glentanar on the Glen Tanar estate in February 1929. With my mother's commitment to her faith I attended regularly over the years, but can now only recall the tedium of the experience. My mother saw the Sabbath as an occasion to don her finery which meant, back in the 1930s, big flowery hats and fur coats. Mother, having lived for some 16 years in the service of the great and the good around the capitals of Europe, had taken on many of their habits and flummery. Dressed in this flamboyant style among the plainly dressed locals, she stood out as a huge embarrassment to me and I learned to dread those Sundays. Gradually becoming braver, I would squeeze into my pal's family pew as long as I was nowhere near the peacock. Whether my attitude affected my mother is difficult to know, but as I got older she only expected me to fulfil about half my commitment. Where she did succeed, however, was to make me very conscious of my failure to live up to her standards and the fact that I had dodged the Victorian expectancy of doing my duty.

By the age of 10 or 11 I took a rather sceptical view of all this paying homage to religion at school and at church. I remember asking my mother why she was so certain in her faith, as she was basically down to earth and realistic in dealing with life. No satisfactory explanation was ever forthcoming, apart from the need to believe, which even then seemed a poor response.

Gentle Jesus, meek and mild, look upon a little child – said every night kneeling by my bedside brings back such memories of childhood bliss. This routine lasted up until I was about 10 when, like my belief in Father Christmas, the age of innocence passed. I was apparently to inherit the same attitude to religion that had so affected my father's early life. Even now with hindsight I am not sure whether his bitter experience, passed on to me so vividly in early childhood awakened my uncertainties. I feel sure that his story triggered an attitude which may have taken many more years to reveal itself.

The attitude to religion of those around me was just to accept it as night follows day. Down through the various levels of society, church attendance was a regular habit, Sunday was a day of rest and God help those who ignored it. My day of decision was fast approaching and with a godfather in the shape of the formidable Lord Glentanar and my mother's unquestioning faith, confirmation could not be delayed for some silly boy expressing vague doubts.

For some six weeks in early 1945, my Saturday mornings were spent in the St Thomas's rectory in Aboyne, being put through my paces by Dean Wattie. I confess to not remembering one fact from all those hours and my vague unease over religion still hung over me like a dark cloud.

On Thanksgiving Sunday in May 1945, at the age of 16, I was confirmed into the Episcopal Church by Bishop Hall in a special service in the Chapel of St Lesmo and if I had hoped the sanctity of the occasion would bring about the lifting of the scales from my eyes, I was sadly disappointed. It was one of those occasions that I have experienced very occasionally when I have felt totally disgusted with myself for lack of backbone. It was not that I had become an atheist or even at that stage an agnostic – I was just feeling confused and uncertain in a world peopled by adults who seemed so certain over something which had the air of the magical about it, which felt so at odds with our practical lives. Having allowed myself to be carried along on the will of others before I was ready to make a considered judgement was evidence that I lacked moral fibre. It was a lesson I was not always to remember on future occasions.

Life through my teens, driven by a sense, not of faith but of duty, still saw me attending church and communion a few times during the year. The Victorian ethic that it was character building to do those chores which you most detested was well and truly burned into my brain. The sense of turning my back on a mother who had invested her life to my upbringing further increased the pressure, so that I felt doubly blessed after my infrequent attendances.

Into married life my responsibility to my children loomed large and they were both dutifully baptised, much to my mother's pleasure. Then for some eight years until they rebelled, I would take them to church and Sunday school. It took little persuasion from them to give in to their dislike of this routine. Both children are part of a generation which feels no need of religion and never seems to give it a passing thought, which makes me wonder how quickly human beings could desert Christianity in the future.

I had entered adult life with a strong sense of the solemnity of the Sabbath and the Christian teachings. Why should I then spend hours both at school and even more so at University, discussing at length the basis for it when others calmly accepted it all?

At university a small band of my fellow students in the Scripture Union wrapped themselves up in daily prayers before lectures and this magnified the problem. Many of these devotees were the more sophisticated and thoughtful, even more intelligent members of my faculty. What drove these young men and women to such devout behaviour in a medical year that was more interested in playing rugby, billiards or poker, and drinking beer and dancing on Saturday nights? Only with much serious thought and research have I unravelled this mystery to my own satisfaction.

"As it was in the Beginning"

"A SOCIETY GROWS GREAT WHEN OLD MEN
PLANT TREES WHOSE SHADE THEY KNOW
THEY SHALL NEVER SIT IN"

— GREEK PROVERB

Glory to the Father, and to the Son, and to the Holy Spirit, as it was in the beginning is now and ever shall be world without end — Amen

This Doxology, or better known as a short hymn of praise, is found in various Christian liturgies and this actual wording is particularly relevant to the Roman Catholic and Anglican churches.

So many of the responses from those Episcopal services are still imprinted on my brain, none more so than the above, which often seemed to herald the end of a tedious hour in prayer on a Sunday. Yet it had a reassuring resonance that sent out the message that all was well with our little world and that we could look forward to another week of peace and serenity.

Throughout my lifetime, some subjects have been considered so set in stone that there is no place to challenge their authenticity. In my childhood, now well over 70 years ago, religion was firmly in this category. For anyone then to question a belief in God was to be pushed to the fringes of society and have the word 'atheist' spat at them with some venom. There is little doubt that Bertrand Russell had religion in his sights, as in my introductory quote, but now with a gradual realisation among many less celebrated thinkers that he was being extremely perceptive, it seems appropriate to consider the implications for our own religious future.

Before proceeding into this world of religions, however, I wish to make clear my use of terminology when describing a lack of belief in the supernatural. Throughout the succeeding chapters I often jump from atheism to rationalism as being one and the same; some readers may not agree that all such terms are synonymous. The term atheism refers to a disbelief in the existence of God, while humanism is a rejection of the supernatural. Pragmatism is the application of the logical mind, while rationalism is a system of belief regulated by reason and attributing all phenomena to natural rather than miraculous causes. When using such terms I am broadly blending them all to mean not believing in anything magical, while preferring to term myself a Humanist or pragmatist rather than that emotionally derogatory term, atheist.

In childhood you give little thought to what is going on around you if it is accepted as normal by the adults. Prayers at school were the norm and to miss them out would have seemed strange. The daily *Lord's Prayer* was repeated thoughtlessly, as were the lines of the well known hymns, liked more for their melody rather than any meaning. Looking back, I am amazed that so much was accepted by all and sundry as reality. No one in my memory ever questioned their beliefs. With little curiosity in the world around them, most people eked out a bare livelihood, which was enough of a burden in itself, without delving into vague imponderables.

Religion was accepted as an integral part of our lives, not to be challenged, as it was all explained in the Bible. Yet, as you mature you realise that the Bible is only a small part and we should be delving far further back to visualise why man has invested so much of his life in this process of worship.

Let us look back to our ancestors, at the recent 'Out of Africa' hypothesis which argues that *homo sapiens* is descended from a small group in East Africa who migrated from that continent 50-100,000 years ago. Human genetics has focused further by isolating the first woman, the mother of this small group from whom we are all descended, calling her Mitochondrial Eve. Life was rudimentary and having evolved over hundreds of thousands of years from more primitive forms, humans had learnt to make full use of nature, had come to terms with life around them in order to thrive. Their hunter gatherer instincts developed, but it would still take thousands of years for man to move on to more agrarian forms of life and progress through the Stone, Bronze and Iron Ages.

Despite recognising the pattern of life, man would not know why night followed day. Why that shiny hot ball shone during the day and at night there was another less vivid ball, which regularly varied in size. Why the seasons followed predictably – why rain fell, why the sea ebbed and flowed. Violent clouds would swirl overhead with winds varying hugely in strength, all unpredictably, driven by some unseen force. Thunder and lightning flashing from the heavens must have seemed like a greater being venting his fury on them, so instilling a belief in forces outside their ken, but never seen. Disease sweeping through the tribe followed by death indicated that they had upset those unseen outside influences.

They watched the birds and beasts reacting to the changing conditions, often long before they had sensed the impending storms themselves, and wondered what gave them those supernatural powers, which were no part of man's armament. Yet the fact that men survived as the most advanced of the primates meant that they had used all their cunning and experience to progress, while other species wilted in the hazardous conditions around them.

Fighting to rationalise his surroundings, man resorted to sacrifices, superstitious rituals and the building of places of worship. Could this be our lot even now, if born on a desert island, without knowing civilisation? We have all bowed down to superstition sometime in our lives. I dodge from walking under ladders, some wear lucky tokens or keep a rabbit's foot under their pillow. Does the wearing of a crucifix denote religious belief or the hope of keeping ill fortune at bay? We have uncanny sensations when coincidences occur, making us conscious of something outwith our ken; or that déjà vu moment when something unusual seems to be happening from another time. Some have premonitions which can have an unsettling effect when they turn out later to happen. To stand in a foreign city and start speaking to a total stranger who has known your father, seems just too weird for chance alone.

Mix those experiences with the odd working of the brain, some people imagining lifelike visions or passing into a spiritual state, and we have the conditions which continue to support the sensation that outside forces are influencing our lives.

All this has been present in our genes from hundreds of thousands of years and is still present today, despite most of the unknowns having been explained. Evolution and discovery have carried us forward to a point almost unrecognisable even to our quite recent Pictish forebears, yet our brains have not been able to discard those superstitious tendencies lurking in the darkest recesses. Praying to the gods goes back to pre-historic times, but it is amazing that today man still needs to bow down to a higher deity.

As a Christian society we have paid lip service to a human being born only 2,000 years ago, which in terms of man's existence would rate as within the last few seconds. Somehow this belief in the son of God persists and although appearing to wane among our young, is still life-encompassing for many, with other world religions also attracting millions. Christian belief is centred around a virgin birth, miracles and a rising from the dead, which would be considered the imaginings of a deranged brain in the individual, but gains total credibility when paid lip service by the masses. We live our lives paying homage to this past master and God the Father Almighty, with no evidence at all that a higher being exists.

Famines and starvation, wars and dreadful deaths are often seen in some way as the hand of God, yet is he chastising us or letting disasters happen to teach us a lesson? Can we discern the hand of God in the way we ourselves deal with the rest of his natural world in a caring Christian fashion?

The unspoken problem in this debate is the fact that we are not all equal. With a few blessed with outsize brains, the majority vary widely in their levels of intelligence, common sense and imagination. Some are blessed to be able to improve their understanding with education, stimulating jobs and contacts, while many are destined to have none of these privileges. Some of us have the facility of open-mindedness, while others are prejudiced, destined to live out their lives unable to open their ears to different points of view.

It is wonderful that we have progressed from small groups of savages to our present state of civilisation, although many seem set on returning to their primitive past with their abuse of alcohol and drugs. Our civilisation has not come about by chance, though, but through advances in science and technology, in a climate of an evolving, ordered society – a society we take for granted, but how does it work? How do all these different humans with their multiple strengths and weaknesses fit into the jigsaw puzzle?

We stress ourselves with thoughts of climate change, the threat to the tropical rain forests of the Amazon and the increasing use of nuclear energy despite the fact that all these measures will never affect those of us who are elderly. Man struggles to pass on to following generations a world that is at least a little better than he inherited it, but his inherent weaknesses and inability to learn from the past often thwart such ambitions.

WHAT ARE YOU - CAT OR DOG?

"KNOWING OTHERS IS WISDOM. KNOWING YOURSELF IS ENLIGHTENMENT"

LAO TZU
Chinese Taoist Philosopher
circa 500BC

Throughout the decades social psychologists have examined our different personalities and how we are likely to function in society. Our various roles in life, from leader to follower, have been analysed resulting in a variety of categories being identified. This can become confusing, so I have dared to simplify a hugely complicated field into two main groups: cats and dogs.

From prehistoric times man has been family and tribally organised. The picture of the male as the hunter and the female the carer of the family and domestic chores is the butt of many bad jokes for our modern generation.

In this tribal setting, living together for the benefit of not only the individual, but also the group, depends on a rigid structure of co-existence. Having too many wanting to lead is just as bad as having no-one prepared to take responsibility for decisions. But evolution has ensured our survival in an alien environment by the development of an array of skills.

A typical tribe would have a leader backed by experienced elders, tasks being delegated down through the ranks, with certain skills becoming evident in different groups. Just as in the animal world, the matriarch may have had a large say, especially among the female members and in bringing up the children. With the passage of time, tribal groups found that survival and prosperity were improved if they amalgamated into ever larger bands, the great proportion of members accepting their role as followers.

In more recent history, the Scottish clans were a good example of tribes linked by common heritage, the members looking after one another, but with a well defined hierarchy of seniority and loyalty to the leader.

How then does the concept of cats and dogs fit into this

structure of human communal living? Take dogs. Through the generations they have been mostly followers - loyal and prepared to conform to pack discipline, the very requirement of men destined to be the followers of the tribal leader. Making up the huge majority of our present population, they are the ones who flock most readily to the colours and die for a cause because their leaders tell them it is just. They make up the bulk of the tens of thousands thronging St Peter's Square or passionately following their heroes in sport, politics and entertainment. They are the backbone of the nation, having multiple skills, but do not want a prominent leadership role and are happy to work essentially for themselves and their family. On the whole they know their place, but can be manipulated by others, as in the French and Soviet Revolutions, Hitler's Germany, or the lynch mobs of the Deep South.

Just like dogs with their dozens of various breeds, so followers are all different with their own characteristics, habits, strengths and weaknesses. Despite this, however, they maintain their basic traits, just as canines do; a pack sense and loyalty to a cause, an institution or a leader, inherited from their distant past.

Who then are the cats of our modern world? In psychological terms the lion depicts the most formidable cat in human society – those individuals who are driven by their inherited or acquired personalities to stamp their authority on lesser mortals. The most powerful figures from history, such as Alexander the Great, have all been lions, while in our own era we have witnessed Adolph Hitler, Joseph Stalin, Winston Churchill, Mandela and Mugabe. Some are motivated by the interests of their community, others are driven by personal gain or fame.

Our most daunting modern lioness has been Margaret Thatcher, while in the commercial world Richard Branson has flaunted his business and showmanship skills. Yet, amongst all these huge cats I must mention the greatest of them all, certainly in our Christian world; a lion which has left his mark on so many of us even today. Jesus of Nazareth, billed as gentle and mild, was nothing of the sort. Entering Herod's Temple in Jerusalem, he threw out all the traders, overturning tables in his wrath: little sign here of the fabled man of peace. In demeanor he may have appeared so, but in determination and self belief he was a giant. Whether he believed he was the son of God does not matter, as long as those around him believed it, so that we still have his life reverberating around us and we continue to sing his praises all of 2000 years later.

Cats of whatever breed, from the mighty tiger to the pampered lap pet, maintain their unique trait, an antipathy to being herded. As a human group they are often described as the awkward squad – always prepared to question and disagree – to walk away when things don't go their way. They can be a huge asset if pulling and leading in the right direction, but a stumbling block to progress if they feel ignored. Among these are the maturing cubs that would oust the leaders, but must wait their opportunity. Cats may make up 10 per cent of the population, but they exert a huge influence.

Human cats, like those in the animal kingdom, come in all shapes and sizes with many different objectives. Modern politics has thrown up a black panther stalking through the dense jungle – the picture I visualise when referring to Gordon Brown as a prime minister. Nearer to home, if you know where to look, you can find lovely furry domestic cats of both sexes, lying in front of their warm fires, knowing exactly which side their bread is buttered on and keeping their cat-like tendencies well under control.

The loners in society are often a bit like our Scottish wild cat – solitary and wanting to be left to get on with their lives outwith the main stream. Also very small in number; said to be no more than three percent of the population and often totally overlooked, we find a breed of cat with its own place in this structure. Often termed the assassin or king maker cat, it is unusual in that although it shies away from leading, it influences events by promoting those it feels are best for the group, or more selfishly, most likely to further its own aims. Hugely supportive of the leadership, this cat is often seen as the closest henchman, yet may be the first to sense when a cause is lost and be prepared to sacrifice the leader and promote a replacement.

History remembers Rasputin as the shadowy figure influencing the Russian Tsar Nicholas II and his wife Tsarina Alexandra prior to the Russian Revolution in 1917. In modern times Alastair Campbell as Prime Minister Tony Blair's closest henchman, appeared to wield similar significant power. The memorable Sir Humphrey in *Yes Minister* and *Yes Prime Minister*, always a step ahead of his boss, the Rt. Hon. Jim Hacker MP, is also characteristic of this particular cat. Mostly shunning the limelight, these cats throughout history have exerted tremendous influence – the power behind the throne – but often unseen and unappreciated.

During lengthy post-graduate studies into group dynamics, my own contrarian attitudes were revealed when I was put into this unsettling group by my tutors, much to the astonishment even of close colleagues. Only by playing back sessions of social interaction were any of us, including myself, convinced that I was indeed a closet Rasputin. Rasputin paid for his behind-the-scenes influence by being murdered in 1916, when it was thought he was trying to get the Tsar to pull out of World War I (1914-18) – and some say it was the British Secret Service who carried out the assassination to prevent this. It is a telling lesson, and odd-ball cats should watch their backs.

Categorising me thus opened the window to many of my strengths and weaknesses, however, and proved a blessing, as I could at last come to terms with myself. My need to write books so late in my career and my wish to express my thoughts and influence others can now be more readily understood.

Psychologists have sophisticated all these groupings over the last few decades, but the essentials remain of leaders, henchmen and followers the world over. We can use this model to gain insight into how individuals, families, communities and nations interact, and also how religions have become so deeply embedded in our very psyche.

The five essentials for leadership are there in the rise of Christianity, as well as that of Hitler. These five criteria are emotional connection, dependency, suspension of critical thinking and dismissal of dissenters, as is demonstrated by the rise of Mugabe as a tyrant in Zimbabwe.

If Mugabe is the example of someone manipulating his way to leadership, then the football fan is the typical follower, whose need is to be associated with someone or something of superior standing. In the case of the fan, the football club —with its aura of importance – provides a sense of belonging and a means of sharing in reflected glory with a mass of like-minded people. The true fan puts up with all the setbacks from a sense of loyalty to the club, but not necessarily to the actual players, the ones doing all the donkey work. Such fans show little insight of football as a sport, only worth watching if it is fulfilling its purpose, to entertain. In other words, football is simply the vehicle selected to fulfil the void left from prehistoric tribal rituals which are no longer part of our society.

The Queen, horse racing as the Sport of Kings and Royal Ascot all provide the rich and trendy an opportunity to display their own special follower tendencies. For the ladies, to see and be seen in the most dashing of fashions seems shallow and unedifying, yet is one of the highlights of their season. I would not wish to be a spoilsport, to deny such people their relaxation and entertainment, but they are little different from the bare-chested football fan, despite their more elevated and prosperous lifestyles.

Differentiating between these groups can at times be very difficult, even in my own family. My mother was very outspoken and of an independent mind, but having often attended Ascot herself, would have been only too happy to have joined in the fashion show. She was very aware of status to the point of snobbery, so I feel she was really a dog, albeit a rather self-willed one. My father, on the other hand, was always the one standing back and observing – the outsider looking in – never a follower, but actually a rather lonely cat.

To the untrained eye categorising can be very confusing. Dogs with particular skills will appear as leaders in their field, while cats with their own agendas will quietly act out the follower role if it is in their own interests. The average person, however, unconsciously carries on his daily life as his inherited genetic code dictates.

Communities, like nations, make up a hugely complex and intricate machine, depending on a mass of cogs to keep them efficient. Leaders are necessary, but even more so are the hordes of lesser beings that make it all happen. The conductor of an orchestra needs his musicians, but the musicians don't necessarily need the conductor, who can always be replaced.

This brings the leadership role into perspective, as only if the followers agree to follow, or are bewitched to do so, can such a lion or lioness be effective. Evolution has been ever so clever as almost everyone has a part to play in society, so that the machinery of life is down to the smallest cog to make it function efficiently.

So where does all this leave us with looking at different aspects of life? This type of template can help you to assess the roles we are all playing in our own little worlds. It partially explains apparently irrational behaviour, and the follow-my-leader tendency of the majority – the taking up of popular ideas, adoration of celebrities and vying to be first to follow the latest lifestyle fashion.

Evolution frequently appears to balance the bonuses and drawbacks in our lives by separating personality, with all our strengths and weaknesses, from intelligence. Some of the cleverest people in my life have been quiet, almost withdrawn, hiding their abilities from the world, while the most outgoing – and often the best loved – have been relative lightweights. Intelligence can play a part by allowing those so gifted to adapt personality to fit their needs.

Whether we are cats or dogs also seems unrelated to our morals. The struggle to do the right thing when faced with the temptation of self aggrandisement appears as difficult for rulers as for peasants. The blatant dishonesty of many African leaders, whose populations are living in dreadful poverty, is the inner battle between self and service. That self so often wins among leaders who themselves have come from poverty is only too understandable. The furore over MPs' expenses in Westminster pales into insignificance compared with the situation in Africa, but the same conflicting temptations exist. All human beings are basically similar. Some of those who become incandescent with rage over others' misdemeanours might behave just as badly if presented with similar tempting options.

The frightening power that leaders can exert over their followers never seems to change, despite our advanced civilisation. A huge proportion of us still fail to think for ourselves, allowing irrational conflicts to continue for years, our minds closed to the stupidity of it all. Much of this is tied into something called faith which has, for instance, kept the bitter rivalry between Catholics and Protestants in Northern Ireland and Glasgow alive for decades. For some of us it appears to be based on blind prejudice from events lost in the mists of time, totally incongruous in this 21st century. African tribes slaughter one another almost routinely, while the Taliban's faith appears balanced by the similarly extreme attitude of the American so-called Christian right. It seems that man is incapable of learning from the past, and that all our primitive drives from pre-historic times are very much alive and well.

Our strengths and weaknesses are what we have inherited from past generations, through no fault of our own. Despite trying to amend our behaviour we are fighting our own natures. Some of us have been born leaders of men, some have been cast as foot soldiers and we must accept our lot. Some have been blessed with magnificent brains, whereas others have been given the minimum, which appears hugely unfair. My only consolation at not being born with a better brain is that my feet-on-the-ground approach leaves me unimpressed with those boasting a Mensa IQ of 150, but lacking common sense.

In many ways we are all like little children at a Punch & Judy show. Those pulling the strings – in government, the business world, religion and the power politics which lead to world wars – are often unseen, and operating to different standards from the man in the street. No wonder we act as lemmings, unaware that we are being treated like these self same puppets.

I personally live with the slaughter of World War I as a lasting memory, from my mother, aunts and grandparents. The unimaginable loss and suffering brought on the innocent through power politics should never have occurred. Those least involved in the decision making paid with their lives, while a handful of people around the world pulled the puppet strings. This lesson is sadly ignored by many of our so-called leaders even today.

TEST YOUR FAITH

**"TO ONE WHO HAS FAITH
NO EXPLANATION IS NECESSARY.
TO ONE WITHOUT FAITH
NO EXPLANATION IS POSSIBLE"**

SAINT THOMAS AQUINAS
13th Century AD

Faith is a word I have been familiar with from my early childhood, but I have never felt very comfortable with it. It always appeared as a way of saying don't think for yourself; there are others out there far better qualified than you, so just believe. There is something very soothing and reassuring about having faith and, being quite an indolent person, I initially took this advice at face value. As the years progressed, however, even my lazy brain started to think this business of an unchallenged faith was asking for an awful lot to be taken for granted.

How I wonder does my average reader respond to a chapter asking him/her to test their faith? Do you immediately know how you will respond? Do you feel it is all too difficult, so please leave me out of the discussion? Some see their faith as a private matter, no business of mine and have I nothing better to do than intrude on other people's minds? Then there are those who wonder why I should need to question something as basic as faith and feel my approach lacks intellectual weight. Why don't I recognise that I am just a half-educated physician who should leave such lofty thoughts to true believers?

A medical training instils a strict adherence to tried- and-tested methods and evidence-based treatments, before the lives of patients are put at risk. The patient may have faith in his doctor or in some higher being, but for the doctor an appearance in front of the General Medical Council would result if he said he had treated that person by something as fanciful as faith.

Many of my medical colleagues, especially of the older generation, could compartmentalise their minds to practising medicine to the highest standards during the week, but then relapse to their devout church-going on a Sunday. Admittedly medicine is not a profession that either stretches or broadens too many intellects; it requires an application of facts, rather than stimulating innovative thought. It is also true to say that being seen to follow your faith with regular church attendance was expected of a profession the members of which were often among the most respected in society. Just carrying on with one's life and not getting too involved in the pros and cons of faith was by far the easiest line to take. In any case it is always an unrewarding argument, as frankly no-one can be certain of the truth.

The faith of patients in their doctors does make me very sensitive to the needs of people under stress, often with the threat of death never far away. Seeing such faith, a silent belief in a higher being, is a very sobering experience. This belief seems not only to engender a more positive attitude to their illness, but to give them an inner strength. Time and again over the years I have been humbled by the quiet acceptance of the inevitability of death with a stoical shrug of the shoulders and the belief that their god would look after them in heaven. For someone who felt no similar certainty, it did make me stop and ponder the great benefit this appeared to achieve, correct or not.

I do not belong to the Prof. Richard Dawkins camp of totally deriding religion and advocating that it should be stamped out of our society. I firmly believe that life is so short and apparently without purpose, other than procreation, that the mind demands something more tangible to hang on to. It is understandable that this perceived vacuum has been filled with thoughts that life is but an entry point to something greater in a better place. Our souls may not peter out in death, but find another home or, as some believe, return in another human being or even an animal. Tales of heaven and hell fire kept the masses under partial control; a rapid decent into Hades was a frightening thought. Better to seeing themselves sitting tranquilly on the right hand of God the Father Almighty.

I would dearly have loved the certainty of a faith in my youth, but even then it lacked credibility. Now scientific discovery is making the continuation of this faith ever more untenable. This is not something I welcome, as despite so much strife being associated with religion, it is reassuring for so many, making sense of a life which otherwise appears to go only to the grave.

I have a lovely image of the past tranquillity of the Church of England, set in the rural countryside, with its pretty church with a fatherly vicar as friend and mentor to all. The community, with the church as their fulcrum, lived out happy modest lives. Always ready to help one another, their belief was based in the goodness and compassion of their god. An idyll that did perhaps at one time exist and certainly was the picture painted for me by my mother, brought up in the early years of the 20th century. Not the image I have of the Scottish Presbyterian Church with its glum ministers and dour congregations, more intent on putting naive sinners on the cutty stool than extending the hand of understanding to the poor and ignorant. This may be a jaundiced view, but in my childhood the vision of the Scottish minister walking through the village in his dark clothing and slouch hat always carried a sense of threat rather than love and compassion.

In the past the average churchgoer absorbed its teachings without much thought, accepting that Christianity rested on proven records from over 2000 years ago. So powerful was this message that adherence was accepted throughout society. Times have changed, with both the thinking and unthinking casting aside the rituals of religion. However, there remains a sophisticated minority who feel the need of the spirituality associated with a faith and draw strength from it in all areas of their lives. They can argue, with tremendous sincerity, as to this and I can almost envy their feelings as I have never been able to sense any such spirituality in my own life.

Some of us are born with an ability to have faith, not only in our religion, but also in one another. This is very honourable, but I sense that in our fast-moving and self-interested world, trust in one another is also eroding. Certainly in my lifetime I have gone from implicitly believing in the leaders of society – and even colleagues – to shrewdly gauging everyone on their merits. No one seemed to need to question our MPs, teachers, doctors, bankers or lawyers in my youth, but increasingly I sense this is not the case.

Faith and trust are not synonymous. I may have trust from personal experience, whereas to have faith I have to surrender my own cerebral thinking. I may have faith in the medical profession from no better evidence than its general reputation, but trust my own doctor from having direct evidence of his capabilities.

In my early days in the NHS patients took it for granted that their hospital and general practice care were excellent, but now I find those around me at times being amazed and delighted when the service proves satisfactory.

Politicians in particular have eroded our faith, not so much in their cash for expenses scandal, as for their patent dishonesty in not telling the public the unvarnished truth. They not only debase themselves, but those in close association, such as our previously revered Civil Service. Our expectance of one another has reduced until we have come to welcome good service almost as a bonus and not as a right. With faith and trust in such short supply in our everyday world is it surprising that the young take less interest in religion?

I have many people close to me, in the family and outside, who work through their faith to help others. This is a blessing and our country would be a poorer place without them. I am aware that my need to delve below the surface of this faith may imply that I am trying to sabotage not only their beliefs, but their efforts in making the world a more caring environment. This is not my purpose and I hope I can show that my position as a Humanist in no way stops me from acknowledging their efforts.

The fall off in church attendances and the ability to recruit to the ministry may not be due to religion alone, but to a changing society which has become more selfish, undermined by a host of services which one can no longer take for granted. In other words, faith itself is under threat.

The Thomas Aquinas quote from long ago tells the devout not to think of questioning church teaching, while isolating those who dare to step out of line. Eight hundred years later this is the message some leaders would prefer to give to the masses, rather than that they should think for themselves.

CREATIONIST OR SCIENTIST?

"WE ARE JUST AN ADVANCED BREED OF MONKEY ON A MINOR PLANET OF A VERY AVERAGE STAR. BUT WE CAN UNDERSTAND THE UNIVERSE. THAT MAKES US SOMETHING SPECIAL"

PROFESSOR STEPHEN HAWKING, born 1942
Physicist and Cosmologist

I consider the idea of a world created within the last few thousand years or so as pure fantasy. However, even in the UK there are small groupings which continue to perpetuate this idea through teaching it to the young. As it features so prominently in the teachings of the Christian Right in the United States, it cannot just be dismissed by a wave of the hand.

I set out in this chapter to consider the evidence against such ideas,. I bear no grudge against the creationists and respect their beliefs, but feel at this stage in our civilisation it is seriously damaging to brainwash the young.

In early Egyptian times it was thought that the earth was a flat disc and it was not until in Greco-Roman times that Pythagoras in the 6th century BC and then Aristotle around 330BC provided evidence that the earth was round. The Greeks, however, continued to believe the earth was stationary and that the stars and planets, including the sun, revolved around it.

Not until the Reformation in the 1600s, with the development of the telescope by Kepler and Galileo, did they ascertain that the earth in fact travelled around the sun. Such suggestions were blasphemous to the Roman Catholic Church and following the publication of *The Dialogue* in 1632, Galileo was found guilty of findings "false and contrary to the scriptures" and was put under house arrest until his death in 1642.

An important piece of the jigsaw was added in 1687 when Newton expounded his theory of gravitational force and the secrets of the universe were beginning to be unravelled. The Roman Catholic Popes, however, continued to ban *The*

Dialogue for the next 200 years. I feel my reference to this on a number of occasions throughout this book is justified, as their attitude to modern life mirrors past barriers preventing progress. History shows right through the ages the dead hand of authority being exerted on anyone or anything which might disrupt their power base, just as today religious bodies refuse to consider that scientific discoveries are eroding the credibility of much of what we have docilely accepted in the past.

There are two recent discoveries worth referring to here when considering the age of the world. Recently a tourist ban has prevented outsiders visiting the Jarawa people on the small islands of Andaman and Nicobar off the south coast of India. The population has fallen to 350, due to their lack of immunity to diseases brought to the islands by tourists. DNA studies suggest that these islanders migrated from the African coast 65,000 years ago.

On Madagascar in 2009, there were studies of eggs of the Elephant Bird, which was 10 feet tall. It was hunted to extinction for its flesh and eggs at least 400 years ago, some say, by French colonists. Another theory is that chickens brought to the islands by humans passed on diseases to which the Elephant Birds lacked resistance, while extensive deforestation robbed them of their natural habitat. The eggs measured three feet long, 160 times larger than a hen's egg. The DNA showed that the bird dated back 19,000 years.

These dates are almost within our ken, but to go back 300

million years to when dinosaurs roamed this earth is beyond the boundaries of human imagination. David Attenborough in his TV series has taken us back millions of years before that to demonstrate the evidence for the first living creatures, yet many remain unconvinced. The finding of fossil remains on the top of Mount Everest is almost unbelievable, while seeing shrimp-like creatures in small pools on the top of Ayer's rock in Australia left me flabbergasted. Let us therefore consider what science has to offer us to negate the idea of a world created in six days.

Most scientists go along with the Big Bang theory, which may be both a positive and a negative. Their explanations after the bang do sound feasible, but they fail to address what went before. Creationists see this as a big flaw in the argument, but the scientists do not claim to have all the answers and are prepared to amend their ideas as more evidence arises. The question as to where did God come from and what existed before him is a line of debate that goes nowhere.

Reading the modern literature, scientists still appear far from certain about the origins of our universe. As one theory is expounded, so other cosmologists and astrophysicists come up with new facts and figures that keep the question in a state of flux. It seems to be generally accepted that the Big Bang over 13 billion years ago established our universe. Cosmologists say that was followed by "inflation" followed by the appearance of "dark matter" which appears to assist in the formation of galaxies. Then they start having problems – mathematical formulae from these theories should mean that our universe should be slowing in its expansion, but instead it appears to be increasing at an ever greater rate. This is all against scientific projections, and has the experts tearing their hair. Now scientists have introduced the term "dark energy" to account for these conditions and more recently the term "dark flow" has been added to try and explain that our universe is but a small part of the whole, which probably includes multiple universes.

Much of this is over our heads and researchers are questioning whether a total rethink and re-evaluation of the evidence is required. The fact that the universe is so difficult to explain should be a sure sign that no magic wand was waved to produce it.

Google tells us that the earth itself is 4.54 billion years old, as determined by radiometric dating. Evidence suggests this is a scientifically accurate figure and not just a matter of theories produced by researchers trying to explain where it came from.

If these concepts are difficult to absorb, the NASA spacecraft to Saturn may be more within our ability to appreciate. Saturn lies 746 million miles away from the earth and has as its largest moon, Titan. For any chance of there being life on other planets and moons, there must be an atmosphere of gases surrounding them, with enough gravity to hold the gases close to the surface. Research had suggested that of all the objects in near space the most like the earth for size and possible atmosphere is Titan. The Cassini Equinox spacecraft was launched in 1997 and in 2005 the probe from the spacecraft was launched and landed on Titan. Amazing photographs from the probe showed river channels and smooth stones, similar to those on earth, which had been rubbed smooth by water or some other liquid. Later, examination of photos taken from around Titan's North Pole discovered what appeared to be a lake. It was evaluated not to be water, but liquefied methane gas – the main component of natural gas. Just as on earth where water evaporates, the methane evaporated into the atmosphere and descended back as methane rain, exactly mimicking our own water cycle.

The fact that on Titan the methane atmosphere probably prevents any known form of life suggests that, with thousands and thousands of moons so far undiscovered, it would be odd if not a few could sustain some form of life with water. Latest research, however, suggests that life forms may after all be able to exist in atmospheres such as methane and arsenic, which opens up a whole new field of possibilities.

Scientists suggest that there may actually be life in a very crude form on one of Jupiter's moons. Europa is the fourth largest of Jupiter's moons and is unusual for its smooth appearance, as against other solar bodies which are pock-marked with craters. This smoothness has been put down to the fact that Europa is a massive frozen lake. Scientists have already isolated micro-organisms from deep down in the earth's ice, roughly equivalent of what is present on Europa, so they are speculating that some very basic life forms could be present out there. Life is moving on apace and our next generation may yet have to face up to even more unsettling extraterrestrial discoveries which will demand a total rethink of all our teachings and beliefs.

Astronomy also has a pressing place in our lives, as the danger of the earth being struck by an asteroid, similar to the one that destroyed the dinosaurs 60 million years ago, is ever present. Jupiter, by far the largest of the planets, exerts a huge gravitational force which keeps its moons and smaller asteroids and debris in place. Because the orbits of many of these asteroids vary, however, the chance that one may come on a collision course with earth is always in the scientists' minds. On Hawaii the telescopes are manned night and day plotting the course of any asteroid appearing too close to earth – a sure sign that no-one is depending on God to save us from another space catastrophe.

It is understandable that human beings feel more comfortable with the magical thought that we arrived out of the blue, totally formed, with multiple species of animals, and plants all in place, created by a supernatural force. A hundred years ago most of us would have believed in such a miracle, despite the fact that Darwin's ideas of evolution were beginning to gain credibility. With every decade producing more evidence of man's ancestry, however, it is almost unbelievable that there are still people who refuse to countenance the fact that humans have evolved from more primitive creatures.

For centuries creationists could justifiably question how life forms came to exist, if not without some god-inspired beginning. Now scientists are able to replicate primitive live cells in the laboratory, the final nail in the creationists' coffin. This advancement is a separate, but unsettling development.

It is really quite bizarre that we still have intelligent human beings obsessed with perpetuating outdated concepts. But remembering that the Catholic Church managed to suppress the evidence of the earth circuiting the sun for 200 years, it should surprise no one that some humans are hard-wired enough to repeat this exercise with creationism for another two hundred.

Some readers may see creationism and their own religious belief as identical, but I think of the various religions as a response to the needs of the human mind which deserve to be viewed with respect and consideration. The creation of the world in seven days, as detailed in Genesis, should be viewed as a hypothesis at a time when scientific evidence was non-existent. While still appearing a reasonable explanation in the Middle Ages, it should have no place in a modern thinking world.

The creationist lobby is all too ready to revise its thinking to fit in to modern discoveries. The universe now comes within their orbit, when only the heavens were included earlier. Then the world that mattered essentially consisted of the Mediterranean, and vast tracts of land were still undiscovered. Our believers are still behind the game in accepting the modern universe, when there is evidence that we may be but one of a multitude. This will not detract creationists from further revisions in the years ahead, while they continue to try to bamboozle us with their mystical, fanciful machinations.

In America a group has introduced the concept of Intelligent Design. In order to get over what they see as bias in not having creationism accepted in schools, Intelligent Design is projected as a science. It is defined thus: "certain features of the universe and of living things are best explained by an intelligent cause, not an undirected process such as natural selection". The intelligent cause is, of course, the God of Christianity. There has been concern that some privately financed schools in England may have Intelligent Design on their syllabus, but this has been denied, although it can be discussed in association with other religions. Along with divisive teachings in some Muslim institutions, this is an area which requires close supervision so that we do not have a core of our future generation maturing as brain-washed young adults.

We modernists in Britain, however, have nothing to feel superior about in regard to our US cousins, as is shown in a 2007 UK poll. Although over 60 percent of Americans still believed in some form of divine creationism, there were still almost 30 percent in the UK prepared to accept this as well – a startling figure for a country becoming ever more secular.

RELIGION –TOOL OF EVOLUTION

❝THE MASTERS OF WORLD PROGRESS ARE EVOLUTION AND SCIENCE WITH RELIGIONS SIMPLY IMPORTANT HENCHMEN❞

PIERRE FOUIN

Language as we understand it appears to have been established about 50,000 years ago. Prior to that, refinement of the vocal chords, along with gradually improving brain function, would have taken thousands of years of imperceptible change. Only with a means of communication could thoughts regarding superstition or religion be shared among tribal groups.

It appears that two schools of thought exist regarding the development of religion. The first is that natural selection was responsible for those most responsive to such ideas thriving in their communities, so cementing a religious or superstitious tradition.

The other school looks on religion simply as a step in man's evolution into the sophisticated beings of the present day. I do not feel there is much difference in either hypothesis, as both are simply part of an array of tools used in the march of progress.

The thought that religion has been simply another tool in the development of man may seem strange to some. Yet there is little doubt that belief in the supernatural was a core part of human brain activity on this pathway of evolution, explaining the mysteries of their world. Rituals to the gods, celebrated through sacrifices both human and animal, gave way to more sophisticated ceremonies, with dance and music added through the latter ages.

The effect on families, small tribes and later on larger conurbations of paying homage to a faith would certainly have had an influence on community bonding, while establishing the power of the priesthood for generations to come.

Is there any evidence then of a religious backdrop which was the stepping stone from our primitive ancestors to the Christian and Muslim faiths of 2000 years ago? Paganism presents a compelling answer to this as it appears to go back to the Stone Age, which would be that period of sophistication of speech from around 50,000 years ago. Paganism, an intriguing study in itself, is recorded as eventually having become the authentic religions of Greece and Rome. The term pagan is derived from the Latin which means a country dweller. A pagan is defined as "having a belief in many gods, but only one is chosen as the one to worship which represents the chief god and supreme godhead."

There is evidence of Paganism, having spread across borders, evolving through the ages of Stone, Bronze and Iron to our present level of civilisation. The positive aspects of this religious development should never be underestimated, while not forgetting the inevitable suffering and turmoil associated with such progress. Hard wired into generation after generation, it is little wonder that the concept of higher forces at work in this huge world became accepted. Only now, with the realisation that our world is miniscule in the universes, do the developed countries begin to question such belief.

Paganism exists throughout the world in small sects such as Druidism. What is more significant is that many modern religions, such as Hinduism, Buddhism and Taoism, are linked to those far off beliefs, as Paganism was based on respect for the environment.

Study of all these faiths and ideas, from way back, suggests a seamless progression from frank superstition up to the gods we worship today. The past of heathens and pagans scarcely fits our modern AD era, however, so man's need to find more acceptable images to worship is surely part of the natural process of evolution, much as it may dismay the devout.

The need for a belief is still of huge relevance, especially in those less developed countries where the masses continue to live in never ending poverty. In areas such as the USA, where social and economic progress seems at odds with a continued commitment to a faith, other factors are obviously involved. Here it may partly be a backlash from a society in which only material things matter. Some in the land of the free want to hold on to old values, which have been ingrained into groups of emigrants from an ancestry of a rigid faith.

Dependency is part of our human make-up so there will always be a proportion of the population who need something to hold on to combat the thoughts of future nothingness. If religion has been a useful tool in the past, then to throw it away now without considering the needs of the devout does seems rather precipitous. True, our present youth do appear unconcerned about their eventual fate, while living-up the good life. Do I sense a feeling around me that deep contemplation by the young is considered fairly pointless, so just let them spend, spend, spend and enjoy life? No doubt our elderly have been voicing similar perceptions down through countless ages.

Speculatively, could this loss of religiosity in our young be the end of this period of evolution, heralding the dawning of a totally new era? The human brain may well be poised to crash through many scientific barriers within which would surely make our beliefs and all the world religions as primitive as ancient paganism.

At present our Christian churches wish to play a significant part in our lives, but seem increasingly caught in a no-man's land of indecision of their role. Modernisation sees the aura of the clerics disappearing as fast as the wearing of the dog collar; pews are removed and pulpits sacrificed in the pursuit of a vague new image. Meanwhile society is crying out for leadership and fresh realistic initiatives to arrest the young from drifting into aimless ways of life. Where are those who can take the best from Christianity and blend it into the realistic world of the Humanist, to benefit our population in these uncertain times?

I have great respect for Dr Rowan Williams, the Archbishop of Canterbury. His gentle approach to life is so reassuring and his lack of dogma has me warming to him personally. He appears to be a man of God, but without the vision of Hell fire if I don't bow down to his authority, which has me applauding him. Can we gently use such men of influence to guide us towards a new vision of religion, whereby the mythical gradually recedes and the positives of love and caring are brought out as priorities? Certainly I do not favour any revolutionary change away from religious belief, but a gradual move towards reality, incorporating all the blessings that we can bring to one another.

I look back on my days in the Boy Scout movement, when

we paid attention to our oath and tried to live up to a set of principles. Today, I still pick up the smallest piece of litter and live my life essentially along those very directives I learnt in the Scouts. Human beings are very malleable and it takes very little good leadership to guide our ways of thinking and doing. Our society seems to be out of control, careering along at a headlong pace to nowhere, and it really does require a sense of national resurrection to put us back into a meaningful orbit.

In the march of evolution, religion has been much like the discovery of the wheel. The significance of the wheel goes back at least 3,000 years BC and over this time it has been developed and sophisticated thousands of times, while retaining its original concept.

Religions, on the other hand, have scarcely changed at all, Catholicism especially remaining dogmatically wedded to the Holy Scriptures. True, the Scriptures are enthralling for theologians to study, but have they any relevance at all to life in this century for the rest of us?

Religions have gone from being in the van of human advancement to trying desperately to hold it back, while keeping man cerebrating about a mysterious world of 2,000 years ago.

The thought that religion may have little relevance for future generations has huge implications for those who try to do more than live their daily lives in a soulless Big Brother box. Some say that our existence, with or without faith will still go on, and for the masses nothing much will change. Birds and bees expect nothing more than a congenial habitat, but man from the outset has battled to make sense of all that is around him and despite the march of secularism this will not suddenly stop. Simple superstition has, over thousands of years, led to ever more sophisticated thought and our present day religions are supported by a welter of profound contemplation.

It is beyond the ability of even our most brilliant scholars to foresee the future. If, however, life does exist beyond our boundaries, what form will it take and will it be friendly or belligerent? Our petty lives with strife among people and nations, especially over religions, will shrivel into insignificance when we come to face the imminent end of our earth, or become exposed to those other worlds in outer space. Survival will then be uppermost in our minds. Evolution will have found a new tool and a new direction in the fight for the continuation of our civilisation.

In summary, religion has been successful through the ages in giving the world a purpose, but now appears to have played its part in this stage of man's evolution. A new era is unfolding with different hurdles to be cleared and where the vision of a god has little credibility. Yes, we must retain all the love and caring, but in a fresh setting. Sad as it is to the faithful to pull the house down, we must when replacing it make sure we incorporate the very best from all those other religions from our chequered past.

WORLD RELIGIONS AND THE MASSES

"RELIGION IS REGARDED BY THE COMMON PEOPLE AS TRUE, BY THE WISE AS FALSE AND BY THE RULERS AS USEFUL"

EDWARD GIBBON, (1737-1794)
Historian. Best known for his work
THE RISE AND FALL OF THE ROMAN EMPIRE

Doctors who bring faith into their repertoire of treatments for patients are not the only group of workers who risk their reputations or peace of mind. Academic researchers are in exactly the same position, with fiction before fact, or faith before reality being the cardinal sins of their profession.

Before leaving the worldwide appeal of religions, I should at least do a little research, as this is an area where most of us have only the haziest knowledge. We still tend to make dogmatic utterances, especially in relation to Islam, so we should at least know the rudiments of that religion and the other major faiths.

The Abrahamic religions of Christianity, Judaism and Islam all appear to owe their origins to the founding patriarch Abraham, whose life is found in the Old Testament book of Genesis. Today, they see themselves as radically different, but that is easy to understand when we view the bitterness that has erupted between Catholics and Protestants.

Christianity is the world's largest religion with about 2.1 billion adherents world-wide. It is said that 42 million people in the UK see themselves as nominally Christian, with around six million actively practising.

The Christian book is the Bible made up of the Old and New Testaments. Jesus was the Messiah promised in the Old Testament, and Christians believe that he is the Son of God, sent by him to earth to save humanity from the consequences of its sins. Jesus gave his life on the Cross and rose from the dead on the third day. Christians believe there is only one God, but there are three elements to this God – the Father, Son and Holy Ghost. Easter and Christmas are the most important holy days in the Western secular calendar.

The Roman Catholic Church is the largest Christian faith

with over one billion members throughout the world, so forming over 50 percent of Christians. Catholics believe the authority of the church lies with the hierarchy of the church and the infallibility of the Pope. Various other differences, such as celibate priesthood, distinguish the Catholic and Protestant churches, with Protestants believing the authority of the church lies within the believer, while disliking the grandeur and display of the Catholic churches.

The broad term Protestant forms the next largest group of Christians, with just under 40 percent of the total. The Protestant faith can be roughly subdivided into Eastern Orthodox, Western Orthodox, Anglican and Protestant, the latter which includes our Presbyterian Church. Outwith these broad categories is a mass of different churches with their regional following, but all based on some form of Christianity.

The Mormons, for instance, founded in the mid 1800s and based in Salt Lake City, were well known for their practice of polygamy. This was discontinued over a century ago, but is still remembered by many. Their church is called The Church of Jesus Christ of Latter-day Saints. They have a membership of 12 million worldwide with 190,000 adherents in the UK. Mormons believe other churches have gone astray and their church is the true church as conceived by Jesus. They have a strong moral stance against many things, including abortion, homosexuality, gambling and tobacco. They are focused on traditional family life and values, and believe that God has a physical body and can have children.

In Mormon scripture the earth did not just appear, but was organised from existing matter. Mormons believe that earth is one of many inhabited worlds, and that there are many governing heavenly bodies, including a planet named Kolob which is the nearest to the throne of God. It seems that amidst all this spiritual presentation there is just a glimmer of reality that our world is not alone.

In my visits to the USA I have been astonished to see the Amish Mennonites of Pennsylvania sticking to their old ways of life and ignoring nearly every modern convenience available to them. Coming to America, this German Swiss Christian sect has even retained its old language and to see families coming into town in their horses and carts and dressed in black, takes us back well over 150 years. Such is their strict faith that they shun the outside world in the belief that this is how they were destined to live.

As a doctor, another sect to interest me is the Jehovah's Witnesses. With a world-wide membership of seven million adherents involved in evangelism, they boast many more millions attending their rallies. Established in the late 19th century, they base their beliefs on the Bible. One of their main teachings is that the world is about to end and will be destroyed at Armageddon. Only Jehovah's Witnesses have any hope of surviving, but God will be the final arbiter. They are best known in the UK from their door-to-door visits and literature.

They refuse military service and are a constant worry to us as doctors, as they refuse to have blood transfusions, no matter their condition. The membership is strictly controlled, and disciplined if they transgress.

Pentecostalism is one of the fastest-growing Christian faiths in the world. With 20 million worshippers in the USA and one million in the UK, it emphasises the work of the Holy Spirit and the direct experience by the believer of the presence of God. It is energetic and dynamic and its members believe they are driven by the power of God moving within them. The religion is based on the baptism of the 12 disciples by the Holy Spirit on the day of the Pentecost. This day marks the end of the Easter season in the Christian calendar and was Sunday, 23 May 2010.

Judaism should probably follow here, as it is a faith coming from the same heritage as Christianity. There are currently around 18 million Jews throughout the world, mainly concentrated in Israel (5.7 million) and the USA (5.3 million). It has been said by some that Judaism is as much a way of life as a religion. Its main differences from Christianity appear to be that it believes in one entity – not, as Christians believe, in Father, Son and Holy Ghost. Jews consider actions and behaviour to be of primary importance, whereas for Christians, belief is fundamental, actions deriving from belief. Jews do not accept the concept of original sin from the Garden of Eden. Judaism affirms the inherent goodness of the world and its people as the work of the creator. Jews are able to sanctify their lives and draw closer to their creator by performing mitzvoth (divine commandments).

Islam is the second largest world religion and the fastest growing, with between 800 million to 1.5 billion in year 2000, and reports that it reached over 1.6 billion in 2009. It represents possibly 23 percent of the world population of 6.8 billion. Mohammed, Islam's prophet, was born in 570AD and died in 632 AD. Born in Mecca, he had many occupations, but his main one appears to have been as a merchant until, aged forty and disenchanted with life, he retreated to a cave in the month of Ramadan and had his first revelation from God. Three years later he began preaching and despite hostility, gathered a large following. With an army 10,000 strong he captured Mecca in a bloodless invasion around 630AD and by the time of his death most of the Arabian Peninsula had converted to Islam. Like Jesus Christ he was a man of peace, which is often overlooked in our Western world where his faith tends to be portrayed as belligerent by its opponents.

Muslims believe it is their duty to evangelise the world to the prophet's message. They are sincere and dedicated in their beliefs, praying five times a day with 17 prayers. In the month of Ramadan, the ninth month of the Islamic calendar, all believers fast from morning to sunset, and give up sex, smoking and any other excess.. They also offer up more prayers than usual and ask for forgiveness of their sins.

The main tenets of the Islamic faith are known as the five articles of faith. The first Article is Belief in Allah as the one true God. A Muslim views the Judeo-Christian interpretation of God with contempt. The second Belief is in angels as instruments of God's will. The third is Belief in the five books of Moses, the psalms, the gospel and the final revelation, the Koran. Muslims claim the Koran has been kept perfect, unlike the corrupted Christian Bible. The fourth article is the belief in the 28 prophets of Allah, Mohammed being the last and greatest, while Jesus is dismissed as a lesser one of the 28. Jesus is thought of as merely a good mortal whom Allah favoured. The fifth Article is a belief in the final Day of Judgement. Only those who obey Allah and his prophet can enter Heaven. Only Muslim martyrs are guaranteed Heaven, while the rest go to Hell, which Mohammed said includes the majority of women.

The main branches of Islam are the Sunnis who make up 80-90 percent of Muslims, and the Shiites who make up the rest. The Shiites broke away from the main body in the seventh century over the question of leadership after Mohammed's death. Both conservative and fundamentalist Muslims believe in jihad or Holy War, but interpret the meaning differently. The conservative Sunnis look on it as a spiritual war, while the fundamentalist Shiites accept it literally.

The majority of Arabs are Muslims, two-thirds of whom live in 10 countries – six in Asia – Indonesia, Pakistan, India, Bangladesh, Iran and Turkey; three in North Africa – Egypt,

Algeria and Morocco; one in Africa – Nigeria. No accurate figure is available for the UK, although it is thought to be about 1.5 million.

One of the most worrying aspects of Islam occurred in 1989 with the Fatwã pronouncing the death sentence by Ayatollah Khomeini on Salman Rushdie for publishing *The Satanic Verses*. A Fatwã is a religious opinion issued by an Islamic scholar, which in the case of Sunni Islam is not necessarily binding, whereas in Shia Islam it is taken as law. This was a hugely damaging decision, with the implication that any freedom of thought can be halted by a threat of death.

Hinduism has grown to be the third-largest religion in the world. It claims about 837 million followers, about 13 percent of the world population, and is the dominant religion of India, Nepal and the Tamils of Sri Lanka, while there are about 1.1 million in the USA. It is recorded as the oldest organised religion in the world, going back at least 6,000 years. Hinduism is not a religion in the same sense as Christianity. It is more a way of life in much the same way as Native American tribes' spirituality is based around a creator, a soul, rituals to preserve their food supplies – all from an age before recognised religions.

Hindus believe that there is one Supreme Being and that the universe undergoes endless cycles of creation, preservation and dissolution. They believe in Karma – the law of cause and effect by which individuals create their own destiny by thoughts, words and deeds. They believe that the soul reincarnates, evolving through many births, until all Karmas have been resolved and liberation from the cycle of rebirth is attained. Not a single soul will be deprived of destiny. Hindus believe that divine beings exist in unseen worlds and personal devotionals create a communion with these Gods. All life is sacred to be loved and revered and so they practice non-injury in thought, word and deed. Finally, they believe that no religion teaches the only way to salvation above all others, but all genuine paths are facets of God's light, deserving tolerance and understanding.

For many, the image of India is oxen roaming the streets unmolested. This is because Hinduism reveres the cow as a motherly figure, a symbol of life, never to be killed.

The other outstanding image of Hinduism is the spectacle of millions of believers wading into the mighty Ganges to receive its blessing. Arising in the Himalayas, the river runs for 1,560 miles through the holiest cities in Hinduism — Varanasi and Haridwar — before reaching the Bay of Bengal.

For me, this river spectacle encompasses the power of human faith, those of us vainly pointing out the fantasy of it all having no more effect than a drop of water in the Indian Ocean.

Buddhism is often listed as the fourth-largest religion in the world, but figures vary from 350 million to 1,500 million. Due to factors such as suppression, non-congregational membership and practicing a mixture of Buddhism, Confucianism and Taoism, definite figures will probably never be produced. Founded in North India in the sixth century BC , many maintain that various Buddhas existed long before that.

Buddhism shares with Hinduism a belief in the law of Karma, with the other facet, the study of Dharma, which helps us find happiness within ourselves. The teachings of the Buddha show a person's path to enlightenment and the fundamental principles that order the universe, along with Reincarnation. This is the rebirth of a living being after death, into a new body, that is either a human, animal, or supernatural being.

Taking a brief look at two other religions does not do justice to all the faiths out there, but this chapter is simply to give a perspective of world beliefs.

Taoism is an ancient tradition of philosophy and religious belief, deeply rooted in Chinese customs and world view. Taoism is about the Tao, which is usually translated as 'the way', but is difficult to define. The Tao is the ultimate creative principle of the universe with all things unified and connected in the Tao.

Taoism originated in China 2000 years ago and is a religion of unity and opposites – the Yin and Yang. A world filled with complementary forces – action and non-action, light and dark, heat and cold. The Tao is not a god and is not worshiped, but Taoism contains many deities that are worshipped in the temples. Taoism promotes harmony and union with nature, along with the pursuit of spiritual immortality. A Taoist practices meditation, feng shui, which is a mixture of astronomy and geography, fortune telling, and the reading and chanting of scriptures. The Communist revolution of 50 years ago destroyed some of the strongest religions in China of which Taoism was a leader, so it is difficult to know how well it has survived under the newer regime.

The Bahá'í Faith is one of the youngest of religions, established in Iran in 1863. It has a worldwide following of six million adherents in 235 countries, with around 6,000 in the UK. The central tenet of the faith is that people should work together for the benefit of humanity, accepting all religions as having valid origins. This welcome message seems an appropriate way to close this outline of religions, but which can be viewed in greater detail on the Internet.

Logic, realism and progress ensure we move on in life making everything out-dated in time. Would we wish to go back to driving a Model T Ford, or even watching black-and-white television? Yet we continue to hark back 2,000 years for beliefs formed at a time we would consider primitive Very strange indeed.

Evaluating statistics from around the world to assess where countries are going with religious belief is very difficult. The wording of various surveys is so loaded with the chance of error, that drawing conclusions is hazardous. However, the differences between the US and UK do appear to be sound enough to illustrate.

"I know God exists and I have no doubt about it" in 1991 had 62.8 percent of Americans agreeing, with only 23.8 percent in the UK. Similar questions about Heaven, Hell, and life after death all produced much the same gap between the two nations. A survey for the UK in 2005 showed that in the age group 12-19 year olds, 65 percent stated they were not religious, while in the period 1983 to 2008, the number describing themselves across the population as non-religious in Britain, rose from 31 percent to 43 percent.

One more interesting statistic highlights the perception that religions are the cause of friction among societies, as well as among nations. A 2006 *Guardian* poll showed 82 percent as seeing religion, "as a cause of division and tension between people". Not a very encouraging finding to end this chapter.

I cannot close however without venting my displeasure at seeing Atheism listed among the religions of the world. To talk about a religion simply on the basis of questioning the existence of the supernatural seems quite ridiculous. If I say I do not believe in Father Christmas, fairies at the bottom of the garden, or pigs that fly, I am simply expressing a realistic opinion which few would bother to challenge. To say I have taken on board the religious belief of Atheism because I find all world religions unconvincing is simply bizarre. I take a point of view, which all around me may challenge, but I have certainly not taken on any new farcical religion to befuddle my readers even further.

IS BELIEF
BLINDNESS?

**❝WHY ARE HUMANS SO DIFFICULT TO TEACH
BUT SO EASY TO DECEIVE❞**

STOIC PHILOSOPHER
Athens 250BC

To further this exploration of religions it is perhaps helpful to take a closer look at the various adherents. The human brain being the driver of religion and not the other way around seems so obvious to me, with the individual's susceptibility to superstition as the most basic component.

Armoured cars are not often mentioned in the same breath

as religion, but perhaps it is time to give them an outing. Prof Richard Dawkins in *The God Delusion* spends an inordinate amount of time firing missiles at the armoured cars of especially Christian faith. My problem with all Dawkins' sniping is, are we identifying the correct targets?

Whether the armoured cars are made by BAE, Alvis, Mercedes or Chrysler and carrying Muslims, Hindus, Jews or Christians makes so little difference. Their purpose is the same, to transport their occupants safely to their destination in some hoped for heavenly resort, while fervently praying along the way. Attempting to shoot up one car may satisfy Dawkins, but it is not the vehicles that are the real challenge, but the conditioned brains inside them. The rifle, like the armoured car, is the outcome of human imagination, but without man to fire it is useless. So it is with our multiple faiths, none of which would exist without man originating them and insinuating them into the minds of the masses.

After all, the majority of religions are not dissimilar in that they all have some mystical message behind them. I contend that their adherents would be the same people, depending on where they lived and which religion was in vogue in that place.

I have never felt the need to thrust my ideas on religion down anyone's throat, not that they would have listened to me anyway. However this is where Prof. Richard Dawkins and I differ; he seems to be on a crusade to convert the religious to atheism, whereas I am simply trying to find my way through the maze of beliefs to come up with a vision for the way ahead.

I recognise the sound reasoning in all Dawkins publications, but I feel he has not explained why some of the most intelligent human beings amongst us continue to reverently pay lip service to something ethereal.

I have had it said to me by the solemnly religious that not only am I colour blind and left-handed, but I have also been deprived of the blessing of belief and spirituality.

I counter my religious colleagues by saying, with tongue in cheek, that possibly my loss of colour vision has been compensated by not being afflicted by a belief in the irrational. However this does raise the question of who is right? The statement that I do not believe in the irrational is not altogether true, as my touching wood and evading ladders shows.

Geneticist Dean Hamer, author of *The God Gene: How Faith is Hardwired into our Genes,* is well worth reading. He postulates that we have all inherited, to a greater or lesser extent, if not an actual God gene, certainly a Faith gene from our ancestors. This goes a long way to explaining our persistent beliefs, despite the march of science.

If we inherit varying levels of faith as Hamer contends, let us start by dividing them into three categories. The first contains the hard wired believers, who would rate nine to ten on the scale. The image to any Scot would be of John Knox thundering from his pulpit on high, bringing hell fire down on the wretched masses. Perhaps this group has inherited the ultimate faith gene which can superimpose itself above their intellect, and which I see as the equivalent of my colour blindness. Much as I used to disbelieve my fellow scouts pointing out invisible arrows on the wall in our trekking games, so they also cannot imagine they have this powerful inborn credulous gene pattern.

My second category contains the majority of the population, with a belief level from five to eight. Their response would depend on the power of their leaders to inspire them. Being mainly followers, they would be more easily influenced. This group is also the recruiting ground for new faiths as shown by the ability of missionaries to convert native populations from thousands of years of their own beliefs to Christianity.

The third group contains those who score one to four on the faith scale, having had their inherited credulous gene gradually weakened through the generations. It contains some of our most highly intelligent people. To understand this it is necessary to study the developing human brain. The child very quickly learns the rudiments of living, which can allow him/her to exist into adult life. However by early puberty the mind, if properly stimulated, can move into overdrive. This stimulation, mainly via intelligence, education and environment, promotes the development of the analytical brain which builds on the more primitive brain to delve into the deeper aspects of life and explore the imponderables.

Thinking back to the chapter on cats and dogs, it is worth

noting that these inborn faith levels appear unrelated to whether the individuals are cats or dogs, leaders or followers.

Cats with fanatical levels of faith will either be the most compelling or dangerous, depending on your point of view. The bigger the blinkered cat, the greater will be the effect on lesser brethren. John Knox would have been a huge cat, but a level ten of faith would have swamped any intellectual ability to see beyond his inherited fanaticism.

Dawkins points out in *The God Delusion* that "the overwhelming majority of FRS members in Britain, like the overwhelming majority of US Academicians, are atheists". For an example of such a person we need look no further than Darwin himself. Destined at one time for the ministry, he came to his conclusions on evolution through study and deep thought, not apparently from a markedly weakened faith gene. It would appear then that those blessed with the greatest intelligence can surmount their inherited superstitions by superior intellects, as long as they have not inherited the irrational levels of nine or ten.

It is proposed that this third group contains those with a weakened faith gene, increasingly being joined by a high intellect group of thinkers. I find myself there by chance through inheritance, whereas Darwin and probably Dawkins himself are there by brain power.

Many of my elderly friends have swung from their passive disinterested belief to reaffirming their religion in the hope of reaching paradise when they die. In my scale, these people have moved from a neutral five or six to probably seven or eight and essentially belong to my group two of followers, just hedging their bets.

I would rate my superstition level at three to four, but depending on my state of mind under stress, it may move to level five, or even seven in the past. As an example of this, I have recently had the root of a large molar removed and although a trivial procedure, it was not without a little anxiety. Driving to the dentist I was stopped at the very last moment by four sets of lights changing to red – this I took to mean a really bad omen for my dental extraction. As it turned out it was a painless procedure in the hands of an expert. It demonstrated, however, my very fragile confidence, when I felt it necessary to find signs from the gods, although I knew it was nonsense.

Mental stress is also a relevant factor in religious commitment. Those under pressure from adversity, danger or unhappiness often have only their faith to bolster them, so it is understandable that prayer and ritual will flourish. Many fishing communities clearly showed how their religion dominated their lives, dictating a way of life so as to have God onside for their constant bitter battle with the elements.

The significance of these ponderings relates to the situation in the UK over the last 60 years. The pendulum of change may be swinging faster than I perceive and already many of our young appear to be rating under five. Whether this lack of religiosity is skin deep and the old inherited superstitions lie dormant is outwith my research, but I doubt that millions of years of superstition will disappear in one generation.

Going from vague uncertainty of my faith, to seeing it as an insult to my rational brain in the face of all the evidence around me, is troubling. I do worry how man will replace his faith and with what in future, as religion does give a certain raison d'être to our lives.

In the broader world perspective, Europe is roughly in step with the UK even in some strongly Roman Catholic countries. Many other faiths lag behind this awakening and the rise of Islam is a destabilising factor which is still not too clearly perceived. Muslims do not appear to see conflict between their faith and an unfolding universe, but this is understandable with huge populations, much poverty and limited education, whereas the American experience is a total enigma.

Americans flock to celebrate their faith in a country much more affluent than the UK, with many in positions of power apparently blinkered fundamentalists. So why is there such a difference? True, the British are more cynical about life, where only the Armed Forces and maybe doctors are held in esteem; America is a nation full of positive thinking, vigour and ambition.

The American religious scene can be quite frightening, with faiths based on handling serpents to all forms of extreme religious symbolism. If ever one needs to be convinced that the average citizen is simply a follower, just view American television or listen to the various religious radio stations.

The conquest of the human mind by such beliefs was dramatically exhibited in 1978 when 914 members of The Peoples Temple – 638 adults and 276 children – under the leadership of Jim Jones committed mass suicide in Guyana; in 1997 in California, 39 members of a sect calling themselves Heavens Gate committed suicide in the belief that the end of the world was upon them.

I feel certain that in the US there is a multiplicity of factors involved in such a depth of belief, including the spirituality of the black community from the past with a number of distinguished leaders keeping their faith vibrant and expressive. The original white settlers brought with them a huge affinity for their religion to the US and they, in combination with the Afro-Americans, have cemented religious belief into the fabric of the state. Whereas in the UK we no longer appear to have a voluble religious leadership, in the US the people are bombarded and bamboozled with all sorts of preachers and public figures using not only the pulpits but the airways to confound the receptive.

Such apparently profound faith therefore appears due to there being so many brain-washed adherents in the US, that the religious pendulum is being temporarily held back. To admit to religious doubt is the death knell for any prospective politician and out into the wider society. Many preachers take Americans for total innocents as they extort money and influence in the name of God, often for their own benefit. This blind faith to the radio and TV evangelists seems so blatantly naïve, it is difficult to relate it to the foremost of our Western nations.

An element of hysteria has been linked with superstitious belief from thousands of years ago among the primitive tribes and this is still present today in certain sects throughout the world. It has been shown that the ecstasy experienced by some from religious involvement is closely associated with the sexual love area in the brain, both appearing to having the attributes of highly addictive drugs. I still recall the Pope's visits to various countries, including the UK, which were surrounded by an almost hysterical enthusiasm. How prevalent it is in the Western world nowadays is uncertain, but there is little doubt it does play some part in preserving old ideas and is an addictive component of the religious ritual.

The evangelist Billy Graham, visiting Scotland in 1955, pulled out huge crowds, including 90,000 to Hampden Stadium in Glasgow. People poured forward to get his blessing as if grasping for some magical potion. Even today on Google you will find people recording the uplifting experience of Billy Graham's rallies as the greatest thrill in their lives. The fact that he was just another human being, but with an aura of the spiritual, completely phased their brains, which only goes to show how easily our minds can be manipulated even in these modern times.

I describe myself now as a reluctant atheist, but an enthusiastic rationalist. This may seem contradictory, but I am sad to see the benefits of religion to whole communities becoming less without something else coming in to replace it. A religion without the mythology is what I probably aspire to, but there seems little chance of that so far.

A picture can tell more than a thousand words, so here is my mental image of our present day. We, of all religions, are gathered together in a very old village hall with the most devout gathered together in the middle, oblivious to everything but their religious ceremonial. Spreading out to the edges are the various scattered groups of the less ferocious believers. On the fringes are the doubters, while at the door are those who think it is probably time to move on. The old roof and walls of the hall show signs of crumbling, which those not totally lost in prayer are gradually becoming aware of. Some non-believers have already wandered off, but it is extremely misty and no one is absolutely sure how to proceed. Some of us wonder what lies beyond our village hall and if there is a place more up-to-date for us all to find shelter? At the beginning of the 21st century this scene has increasing significance for man, perhaps increasing in tempo throughout the next decades.

Those of us who feel we have moved on from blind faith are, however, venturing out uncertainly into a world where the landmarks are poorly signposted. Religion was a cosy home for us and we could nestle together to give mutual comfort in the name of God. Now, there is no clearly defined path to follow, so we drift carelessly across the landscape doing as we wish, with no spiritual direction to guide us in our responsibilities, within and without the family. These are difficult times – not for me in old age – but watching the young following the cult of celebrity, materialism, self interest and a certain soullessness gives rise to anxiety. It seems somewhat ironic that we who question the rationality of Christian belief should be looking back and seeing it as an age of at least some certainty, while rather dreading what may lie ahead.

THE PROS AND CONS OF ATHEISM

"IN SOME AWFUL, STRANGE, PARADOXICAL
WAY, ATHEISTS TEND TO TAKE RELIGION
MORE SERIOUSLY THAN THE PRACTITIONERS"

JONATHON MILLER, born 1934
Physician, author, theatre and opera director, humorist and sculptor

An atheist is defined as someone disbelieving in a god and is a term with heavy overtones of something really sinful. To my generation of oldies it holds an ominous threat of being cast out of decent society, but this association is not the same for our young people.

Throughout my life it has never been easy to accept that I am in this category. For years I hid behind the term agnostic until I came to realise that this was the same hypocrisy that I levelled at many of my colleagues, who paid lip service to their Christianity. However, I believe that disowning a god is hugely difficult for many as it flies in the face of accepted belief over generations. Only now, by beginning to see religion as a stepping stone in the mental development of man, can we hold up our heads and feel no remorse for our seeming betrayal. Others elect to accept the old teachings because we have brains that are differently programmed and genetically sensitive, and we exert personal choice.

Faith must give the way-out religious sceptics amongst us a field day, as so much seems beyond the bounds of reality.

Through the latter centuries, questioning religious belief was left mainly to those of a high intellect and philosophical mind. Certainly what appears in print comes from such scholars and was a hazardous initiative as it brought down the wrath of not only the all-powerful churches, but those in local and national lay control. With such adversaries, those propounding this advanced thinking were easily denigrated to the populace, so that it has taken up until recent decades for the ideas of Darwin to be properly recognised, developed and accepted by the common man.

The realist from the past required an analytical brain, clarity of thought and a level of intelligence to evaluate and untangle all the arguments for and against faith.

With a religious upbringing, commencing in the cot, the human brain has been exposed to the acceptance of supernatural events as reality from the outset. In a Christian home, church and school, huge influences are exerted on the young mind to accept such teachings and it takes a strong, intelligent individual to keep things in perspective. The atheist has had to battle against popular biblical images and struggle against antagonism to think for him/herself without support.

The pendulum began swinging towards freedom of thought in the UK following World War II. The cloying influence of the Church of Scotland was certainly weakened in my district with the disturbing influx of Roman Catholic evacuees, their rituals and different observance of the Sabbath clashing with the dark Presbyterian ethic. The war itself loosened society norms and the experience of civilians and the Armed Forces left many in doubt over the role of a caring god.

In our own modern times, the weakening of the church in Britain however does not, I feel, come down to a sudden bout of realism among non-adherents. The power of the church in the past has been its ability to make people feel they are out of line if they did not conform. With the majority prepared to accept this, the odd drifter and non-conformist could experience an uncomfortable life. Once the drifters multiplied, however, then more and more could quietly turn their back on the drudgery of the Sunday sermon. These dropouts were not driven by serious contemplation, but mostly by laziness, boredom or deciding on other priorities. It is little wonder that they still aver to be Christians, but find church-going of little or no importance. I can understand their apathy, but do not consider them as being other than floaters who, going with the flow of life, are influenced more by the fashion of the times than any deep thought.

Just as the religiously committed are usually steeped in their faith, true atheists and realists have had to come to terms with their stance from difficult and often unsettling thoughts. Atheism is no easy opt out, requiring determination in a climate that often considers such assertions sacrilegious. Community support and a faith that someone is out there with your interest at heart, are not easy benefits to surrender, especially when faced with adversity.

Remembering the cats and dogs, most drifters will be found in the dog kennel, while the awkward squad of cats will be the ones to twist the religious tail. In other words those who are predestined to be followers are not the most likely to be in the van of teasing out the incongruities of religious faith.

My father, despite being poorly educated initially, showed huge insight in seeing Catholicism as the bully boy in dealing with the poor French peasant farmers. This at a time when such an opinion would have had him excommunicated from Rome was a powerful message to me to think for myself. His rebellion was not nurtured in a hotbed of discontent, as the peasantry just accepted the priest's omnipotence, but was very much a personal response. It is little wonder that this particular trait has been passed on to me, as in other fields we are only too aware of children inheriting their parents' intellects or sporting skills.

A troubling problem for any atheist is to answer why we are here and what for. What does the future hold for the human race and are we all just involved in a merry-go-round of doing what generations of our forebears did, but in an ever more sophisticated fashion? This sense of aimlessness in our existence must be much worse for the realists amongst us than for those who feel we are living in the hope of reaching the Kingdom of Heaven

So does atheism bring anything worthwhile to our lives and help us face the future more perceptively? Church-going in my childhood was not a particularly enjoyable experience, but as an Episcopalian was not quite as dour as the Presbyterian faith of my friends. There was certainly never the happy-clappy atmosphere of the West Indian tradition or the wonderful singing of African congregations. It never struck me that religion was supposed to be happy and so the intense seriousness of the atheist cause came as no surprise.

Atheism is certainly not a light hearted topic and seems to be projected by people with the cares of the world on their shoulders and scarcely a spark of humour in sight. It appears to rubbish the opposition without much evidence of insight into the uncertainty it may be causing. The harsh truth for the atheist cause is that yes, it probably is all correct, but it is having no beneficial effect, other than to undermine the power of the churches and unsettle their flock. It does not appear to be improving the lifestyle of the population, either practically or mentally, so where is it leading us? Depriving the young of the civilising atmosphere associated with the religious life style, is atheism a destroyer of communities?

On the other hand, in the UK where church-going is a minority priority and where the markedly religious are increasingly viewed as old fashioned, does it really matter? The oppressive religious constraints of my youth have passed and my own children appear no worse of not having had a religious upbringing.

Enter Christopher Hitchens, the well known English writer and pundit living in New York, to further muddy the waters of atheism. He talks of the "new atheism" which differentiates the atheist who quietly wishes that belief in god was correct, from himself and his followers who term themselves antitheist or anti-theist – someone who is relieved that there is no evidence for such a concept as a god. He argues that the idea of a supreme being is a totalitarian belief that destroys individual freedom and that free expression and scientific discovery should replace religion as a means of teaching ethics and defining human civilization.

This leaves me in a quandary as I believe religion has been

simply a tool in man's development, but much that it has spawned in human nature and the community of churches has been beneficial. I would therefore be happy to see many such benefits conserved in a more realistic atmosphere. Does this then leave me in a no man's land, wanting to retain such benefits but agreeing in principle with Hitchens' conclusions?

From the evidence I see around me locally, those of strong religious faith are uplifted in their lives in both their prayer and in living a caring Christian existence. In so many ways I envy them their diligence, but then have to remind myself that this is what evolution is all about; for those breaking the way into a more realistic future, nothing will ever be easy.

I disagree with many Christians in their assertion that without a religious upbringing the young are in danger of entering a moral vacuum where all the civilising benefits of church teaching are lost. I agree such teaching is valuable, but as a parent I have taught exactly those values, as I am sure every other intelligent atheist aspires to do. There seems little evidence that our modern generation are any less aware of good and evil. Example before dogma is probably the telling factor.

For years, despite my doubts, I could not get past saying I was an agnostic. Chambers Dictionary defines an agnostic as "one who holds that we know nothing of things beyond material phenomena" – in other words, nothing is proven one way or another. This is a very convenient way of not upsetting the religious by leaving it open to conjecture that perhaps there could be something surreal out there. I found this a cosy position to take up among my friends, but through the years I have had to steel my heart to come out and recognise the lack of credibility of such a position.

Can we preserve the positive strengths of Christianity while casting off the mythology? Without a faith are future generations being denied the possible highway to worthwhile lives, so descending into an aimless life of self indulgence?

Finding the new way ahead, some of us must feel like John the Baptist, but so far we have still to be blessed with his vision. Our world in many ways changes slowly and with human life limited to a few decades, none of us are around long enough to see the effects of our thinking. For me the journey has been hugely fulfilling and I do not regret for one minute my progress from Christian to agnostic and now to realist – however not a journey I would advise for everyone.

To summarise then, as a realist, I have to accept that atheism is a rather miserable doctrine in that it bears no obvious benefits for the ordinary UK citizen who finds succour and reassurance in a religion. World wide, of course, religions have serious ramifications as witnessed in the USA where its zealots are rated as dangerous as the Taliban, so a little caring atheism here would be of huge benefit.

Man is evolving and becoming more sophisticated every day in the material world, but appears to have run into the buffers as regards why he is here and what for. Until our best intellects can find a new direction and purpose in life, the mass of humanity will find itself in limbo if we come to undermine all faiths. Not that this will occur for generations, but if the world survives a few more thousand years evolution has to start coming up with some answers to give human life some further meaning.

Unfolding scientific research might give us just a glimpse of the future and the concluding chapters of Dawkins *The God Delusion* are well worth reading. Here he considers quantum mechanics, a branch of physics that deals with discrete invisible units of energy called quanta. Hugely difficult for the peasant in me to understand, I still remember the science fiction TV series *Star Trek* and the "Beam me up, Scotty" teleporting command that enthralled us all. Already scientists have accomplished this on a small scale, so perhaps we are about to enter a whole new, exciting field of evolution where religions, like bows and arrows, will simply belong to a bygone age.

I have been asked how I feel living among so many practising Christians without challenging their faith. I always answer that I am delighted to witness their thoughtfulness and kindness and almost envy them their unwavering certainty. Then, however, I have to admit that I feel like the little child at a party, with all the other children fervently believing in Father Christmas, when I know that behind the flowing white beard and red cloak is our friendly next door neighbour.

PRAYER – IS IT WISH, WANT OR INSURANCE?

••PRAYER IS THE LANGUAGE OF A MAN BURDENED WITH A SENSE OF NEED••

EDWARD M BOUNDS (1835-1913)
American Methodist Minister and
Civil War Prophet of Prayer

Over the trillions of hours of man's endeavours throughout the ages, the time spent in prayer and reflection might not be so far behind. To holiday in a Muslim country brings home, in a striking manner, the importance of public and private prayer, at least five times a day, having been summoned with such ringing gravitas.

Prayer has existed since man's brain first started to battle with all the imponderables surrounding him. Prayer belongs to what I term the "wish/want" centre of the brain. Right from the day the baby in the crib reaches out for his rattle or comforter, to the day he passes away hoping for tranquillity in heaven, the mind is grasping for something, real or imagined.

In childhood, our little brains quickly become attuned to wishing. Whether it is for affection, attention, food and drink or to the lovely toys in shop windows, our lives are enveloped in this need. Wishing and praying simply went hand in hand in my youth. In the 1930s, despite so much being beyond the ability of our parents to provide, the desire to have things was never diminished one iota.

Introduced to the world of prayer in the home, church and school, I rapidly turned to praying fervently for the gods to deliver me a wish list of exotic toys. Widening this out into other fields, I would pray to reconcile my parents from their last worrying row or to make Sunday pass more slowly, so that school on Monday would be kept at bay. Praying to the Lord to look down on an indolent little sinner and allow him to pass his exams was an ever present plea. At no time did I think of this as incongruous, while not really expecting my requests to be answered. It seemed so natural to pray that it did not occur to me, until years later on, the absurdity of it all. Even in my early years at university I could still turn to prayer as the hand of retribution came ever closer to me for my lack of industry. Only when prayer failed to stop the juggernaut, did I sit up and say to myself – "Grow up".

Over the subsequent years praying to a god has been jettisoned, but I have still that superstitious habit of thinking there are devious influences trying to manipulate my life. I intuitively touch wood and insist on exiting the same door as I entered, while the thought of seven years' bad luck breaking a mirror has me on tenterhooks. Under the surface of my apparent common sense approach to life is a much darker side, which harks back to my early ancestors.

Entering our modern world of the last few thousand years, various religions have emerged having retained primitive customs and mystical rituals. Much prayer has been amended to suit the times, but remains a core component of most religions.

So what is the significance of prayer and what is it achieving or hoping to achieve, if anything?

Looked at from the rational point of view, one must wonder at the hours spent in supplication without any obvious return. The fact, that on the face of it, all this prayer achieves nothing that can be measured or witnessed, flies in the face of man's need for evidence and practicality in his life. Yet, believers continue to attend their churches, offering up their prayers, without any concrete evidence of response from the gods.

Some faiths regularly pray for the second coming of Christ, some for the end of the world, without any indication that their beliefs will be fulfilled. Many Christians perhaps see their diligence as their insurance policy to entering the kingdom of heaven, which is at least a reason one can almost comprehend.

Belonging to a massive fraternity with so much power and influence is a cosy haven for many, as we hope to gain all the benefits, religious and practical.

In my youth some of the most mean and inconsiderate people I came across were not only regular church-goers, but often involved in church affairs, even annual visits to the General Assembly of the Church of Scotland in Edinburgh. Living a dual life of total self interest during the week and fervently praying and donning the Christian halo on Sundays made the whole religious experience a charade. However, such adherents would feel their piety on a Sunday was penance for a week of self indulgence.

If the object of prayer is all ethereal, then for Humanists it would appear a harmless ritual, if not a very rational one. It would be churlish of the atheist, however, not to recognise that prayer has also an altogether different aspect. The comfort derived from prayer cannot be easily dismissed and I recognise the benefits, if not the logic. Prayer opens up another world from the realism and selfishness of every day living. Prayer allows quiet contemplation, when we can accept that we are not perfect and can regret and ask forgiveness for our sins and omissions. Thinking of others and extending the hand of friendship and thoughtfulness through prayer to those in poor health or reduced circumstances is a touching ritual. Prayer can give strength in adversity, allowing believers to pray for the safety of loved ones in danger. There is really nothing else to replace such a need; I am so aware of this having experienced it often in the care of patients.

Even as a realist I am always greatly humbled by the image and intensity of the individual at prayer. Also the calm reassurance of a nation with its heart and principles in the right place as we pay homage to our war dead is hugely impressive.

That the various tragedies of life can be saluted and remembered in a communal context is also of great importance; without prayer it is difficult to imagine any other form of service capturing the solemnity of the occasion. It is easy to denigrate the apparent uselessness of prayer, forgetting how much it is at the heart of showing that individuals, families, communities and nations can still consider and remember others.

As a Humanist I have to admit that the ritual of hymns and prayer at a service for the dead, in the setting of a church, continues to transmit the spirituality I associate with such a solemn ceremony. Somehow there is a lack of atmosphere in the Humanist funeral which I feel comes down to the fact, that despite my views, the Christian environment continues to be part of my being. Nowhere am I better shown to be caught in this no man's land between belief and realism than in my still feeling reassured by the sense of calmness and peace derived from a church and its service. Little wonder, then, that those of us brought up in the faith have difficulty in coming to terms with our intellects.

As with so much in religion, it is not the act of prayer that is astonishing, but the millions voluntarily engaged in such a regular ritual. The grace said before meals brings back so many happy memories of school life, while the vision of American families joining hands together around the dining table to steadfastly say grace on a daily basis, is somehow so reminiscent of the more innocent times of the early settlers.

Memories of my grandchildren aged around five attending a Roman Catholic school, insisting on grace then solemnly crossing themselves before eating, despite their parents belonging to no religion, showed how easily the human mind can be drilled to conform. I think it does us no harm to stop for a moment to appreciate how fortunate we are in life to have enough to eat and drink, but I do wonder if for the majority the prayer becomes yet another meaningless act.

The ritual of sportsmen and others as seen so frequently on our televisions crossing themselves before events, I feel, is also down to simple superstitious habit for most.

How then are we to judge and assess the impact and usefulness of prayer? The awesome spectacle in the Middle East and other Muslim countries of the populace in prayer is fascinating, but also extremely frightening. Human minds controlled by such mysticism makes one wonder why we were born with any independence of thought, when outside factors can control them totally. I feel very anxious that this brain washing of a whole population could be manipulated as much for evil as for good. True, our civilisations demand that to prosper we live in harmony to fit in with society, but surely this does not require subjugating our whole being into the realms of the supernatural.

As a realist, I am convinced these religious beliefs and rituals are erroneous, but are tolerable as long as they pose no threat to other people. Christianity has gone from being a belligerent religion, as demonstrated in the early days of the Crusades, and then throughout the ages, only now to be seen as a fairly tepid faith which few can really revile in the UK. Other faiths are not so docile and have the power to be an increasing problem in the future.

In the final analysis, anything which stops us in our tracks to pause and consider others is a good thing. If it goes on to actively assist those who have been prayed for, that is a huge bonus. If prayer has to exist under the cover of mythology, then I for one am prepared to accept it as a price worth paying.

HAS CHRISTIANITY A FUTURE?

"NOT ONLY IS THERE NO GOD, BUT TRY FINDING A PLUMBER AT WEEK-ENDS"

WOODY ALLEN,
born 1935
Screenwriter, director, actor, comedian, jazz musician and author.

In the literature for and against religious belief there is a dearth of discussion as to what the future holds for Christianity. Believers paint a rosy picture of continuing faith, while the atheists foresee an ever weakening following, both from disbelief, but mainly from disinterest by our younger generations.

Church going is still a very gentle way of passing a Sunday and one is mostly surrounded by people who would see themselves as good citizens and conforming to a way of life which shows their proper upbringing and caring outlook on the world. Congregations, however, depend on the middle aged and elderly and this is ringing alarm bells across our established churches. Not only are congregations under strain, but so is recruitment for the priesthood, which must have serious implications for the future. Church funds keep falling affecting the ability to maintain buildings, while stipends must inevitably battle to keep up with the general standard of living.

Although we may be decades, even generations, away from the demise of the Christian faith, it must be reasonable to look at whether it requires a serious rethink to bring it into harmony with, if not the 21st century, then certainly the 22nd.

In another chapter I have painted the rosy picture of an English rural scene of the past with the church at the core of village life and the kindly vicar ministering to his simple contented flock. This comes from my mother's experience back at the end of the 19th century and is something I have always envied. I would happily put my thoughts on atheism on hold to recapture that idyllic way of life. The modern bustle with the feeling of the devil taking the hindmost with money and pleasure uppermost in so many, has certainly replaced such memories. The realist in me knows that hardship and suffering were so prevalent in those far off days and that it is all too easy to be sentimental for an existence which was far from blissful.

I have a great respect for past history and tradition and so my thoughts on the future of Christianity are steeped in far more than simple faith. Faith has been the cement holding the whole edifice together. All sorts of different materials are being held in place, achieving a far greater effect than the cement on its own. Within the framework whole communities have coalesced for the common good, spreading out to give moral leadership, comfort in common prayer, music, and a host of social activities. The Church has radiated caring, while providing the message that there is a purpose to life which has cheered and reassured millions throughout the ages.

Whether we believe in the basic concept of faith or not, this has been our heritage and to cast it aside unthinkingly is unacceptable. I feel uncomfortable seeing churches being converted into houses, but am dismayed when they convert to cafés or business premises. I well recognise that this is probably inevitable but the sense that what was once a building of worship, no matter how mistaken, is now converted to the practical world, seems totally incongruous and somehow blasphemous, which just shows I have not shed my Christian upbringing after all.

So how does all this relate to bringing the Christian faith more up to date and facing up to a totally different world from the times of Jesus Christ? A head in the sand attitude I feel sure may doom failure for at least our Protestant faiths, while

Catholicism with its more dictatorial and subservient approach may hold its adherents for somewhat longer.

Without wishing to go down the Dawkins route of challenging all the teachings in the Bible, it would interesting to see what atheists might be prepared to accept to continue the great benefits of the Christian message.. We recognise that the Bible is a collection of thoughts, memories, writings and a great deal of hearsay, none of which can be accepted without a degree of scepticism. After all, we have learnt in modern life to reserve judgement on all sorts of information, whether in our media or from the neighbour next door. Certain people have an interest in presenting facts to suit their own interests, as is all too obvious across the spectrum, especially in the world of politics. Two thousand years ago the same distortions, lies and imaginings would have vied with unsullied truth, so it would be naive to believe too much of it without question.

To try to accommodate flexibly-minded atheists with their counterparts in the Christian faith is probably a step too far for both parties.

Apart from Adam and Eve, my first problem as a doctor is with the virgin birth. In my early career before the era of the pill, I was also presented with the virgin pregnancy. These ladies – always unmarried and adamant in their belief – were at times hard to disbelieve, until a sly word from a neighbour would undermine all the tears and protestations.

Joseph and Mary were married and being humble people

the most natural outcome would be a family. Without the benefit of DNA we shall never know whether Joseph had any input into this virgin son, but it stretches credulity to the limits to believe this was other than a natural outcome for human beings.

Miracles are also hard to fathom. Have we ever heard of or come close to a miracle in our lives, or been aware of them in the lives of our ancestors? Yes, many odd occurrences, not least in medicine, which defy evidence, but the word miracle is generally accepted as mythology. The human brain cannot cope with the sleight of hand of the conjuror or what appear to be impossible feats. But they can all be explained by those who appear to have the magic touch. Miracles throughout history have depended on individual reports and in medical experience are looked on simply as contortions of the mind. Miracles as an analogy to symbolise events are understandable, but only as illustrations.

Jesus Christ, presenting himself as the son on earth of God Almighty, raises the question: did he believe this, or was it sales pitch to further his image as the most powerful prophet in the world? Again many disturbed minds project themselves as John the Baptist or Napoleon, but usually find themselves firmly in the hands of the psychiatrists. From the records, it would not appear that Jesus was in that category, so it is uncertain what lay behind his conviction of being the son of a god. Such an assertion seems today as unlikely as finding fairies at the bottom of my garden.

In Islam, Jesus is regarded as one of a number of less important prophets and nowhere near the level of Mohammed. Were there many so-called holy men, vying with one another in importance in an age when the reasons for life on earth seemed totally obscure? Jesus and Mohammed have stood the test of time and have outlived other holy men in the religious stakes, but does that make them any more credible than those others who have been lost in the mists of past generations? Jesus as a caring holy man – yes, but as the son of God sounds uncomfortably like self promotion.

The Resurrection just goes too far for realists. The evidence is dependent on a few closely involved adherents and lacks real credibility. Human minds can be manipulated into believing anything if peddled strongly enough, especially if surrounded by superstition and black magic. One has only to look back to the Middle Ages in our own district when witches were regularly burnt at the stake on the whim of those around them, suggesting some spurious magical event. Christianity required these magical attributes to get its message across and attract a following, in keeping with modern day slanted publicity. Superstition and belief in the unknown were basic constituents of life, so claims of miracles such as Jesus being the son of a god, and the Resurrection would have impressed innocent minds.

The really startling fact is not in the story of Jesus, but that such impossible claims could still be believed in this 21st century. In Darwin's era the clouds of uncertainty over man's existence began to disperse, but it has taken up until the middle of the 20th century for the penny to drop that a story two thousand years old should be seriously called into question. Such, however, is the power of faith that only now is man beginning to emerge from this fantasy world.

So could non-believers be influenced to see merit in our Protestant and Anglican faiths if certain of the mystical influences were phased out? I am aware that some senior churchmen already question one or two of the main tenets of the faith, which seriously undermines their hopes of projecting their teachings to a more questioning generation. They already perceive that the young find much of the religious message bizarre.

For me the previously detailed areas of beliefs cannot be preserved other than as teachings from the past. We may all have an inner god we answer to, that we probably recognise as conscience, which I can relate to. Otherwise the teachings of Jesus are worthy and can still be relevant today. If the church used the Bible as the story of Christian beginnings, much as we teach the history of our nation, but then applied those teachings to a modern realistic world, we could preserve all the benefits that ripple out from Nazareth.

Listening to the Archbishop of Canterbury gives me a glimmer of hope that some common ground can be found where love and caring for one another become the priorities to overcome our different perceptions of life. Much of his scholarly approach to theology and his deeper thinking are out in a rarefied atmosphere where my intellectual oxygen begins to run out, but leaves me hugely impressed. Is it asking too much for our finest religious brains to begin to give their flock some true leadership for the future with a more enlightened modern approach?

Any collaboration between atheist and Christian requires a huge leap forward in the thinking and imagination of both sides. Knowing many clerics and congregations throughout the years, the merest change in even the format of services or hymns brings a deluge of protest, so any progress is hard to imagine. Listening to the average prayers, blessings and wording of the hymns, they are so far removed from reality that we probably need two further generations before the churches shake themselves free of mythology; but then, sadly, it may be too late.

Tackling the problem by downgrading dog collars and removing pulpits is purely cosmetic, when the true cause is far more fundamental. Indeed doing away with the glitz of tradition may be hastening the demise of the church, making it appear as just another service provider. Small mindedness and lack of vision are stifling any chance of more expansive thinking while the continuing emotional preoccupation with the ordination of women and homosexuality does appear as fiddling while Rome burns.

Understanding that religions are simply a part of man's evolution, that the Bible is a historical record of its time and that we should be building on its foundations to preserve the principles of love, understanding and fellowship seems obvious. Instead, the human race as a whole is still wedded to outdated mythology.

Being a realist is certainly no fun. The feeling of exasperation when running in to the stone wall of institutional religion is so very depressing. This is aggravated by the dismissive attitude of many atheists, projecting those who still believe as intellectually backward, which does not further the finding of an acceptable compromise.

Change will only gain pace very gradually and will require strong, open-minded leadership. After two thousand years of offering praise to an unseen, imagined deity, it is asking a great deal of our religious leaders to tackle reality. Vested interests are at stake, making sure the status quo is maintained to the bitter end, especially in the Vatican. To me it will be so sad if rigid minds fail to see the problem ahead and eventually future generations become deprived of the many valuable teachings of Jesus Christ.

CATHOLIC PRIESTS – A CHARITABLE VIEW

"THE POWER OF MAN'S VIRTUE SHOULD NOT BE MEASURED BY HIS SPECIAL EFFORTS BUT BY HIS ORDINARY DOING"

BLAISE PASCAL (1623-1663)
Mathematician, Physicist and Catholic Philosopher

It may seem odd that I should start off talking about charity and immediately turn to the Vatican. For me the Vatican holds the image of a faceless, powerful empire ruling its flock with a rod of steel and having its doctrine implemented by a regiment of overweight, self-satisfied priests. This is probably due to my father's perception of the papist faith from his childhood, passed on to me in my early years.

Over the years I have refined my ideas and have experienced much interest and kindness from many of the brotherhood. However much papal doctrine, such as related to contraception and abortion. does not sit easily with my experience of the needs of ordinary people, and so I still have severe reservations about Catholicism. In addition, the revelations about the abuse of children by priests over many decades makes for sorry reading and has affected thousands of children's lives into adulthood.

The Vatican is a vast business empire with its heart in Rome, but its tentacles reaching out throughout the world. Electing the Pope to be God's leader on earth seems a really wonderful con trick, but is swallowed by the faithful around the globe. How any man, chosen from among his own inner circle, can be said to be a representative of an ethereal being defies credibility.

Living in an increasingly secular society like the UK, exposes the average citizen to all the conflicting arguments about religion. Despite this and the vigorous attacks waged on it, a large number of seemingly intelligent individuals continue unwaveringly in their faith. Is it any wonder that ordinary Philipinos when interviewed come across as little innocent children in seeing the Pope as God on earth? It is frightening and rather endearing to see such an enduring faith at first hand, while we ourselves live in an increasingly cynical, materialistic world of our own.

My own experience of the priesthood goes back to the dark days of World War II when hordes of east-end Glasgow children descended on our rural oasis on Deeside in Aberdeenshire. Coming to the estate of Glen Tanar, some were housed with local workers while the main body of boys were accommodated in converted stables, with the dormitories in the hay lofts and the kitchen and dining rooms set among the horse stalls. Their education was carried out in the local recreation hall and their wild, boisterous presence changed our little world for ever.

Overseeing their lives were half a dozen young priests and they turned out to be delightful people. The bond of mutual respect with their young charges was hard to believe, with boys used to the chain and razor gangs of Glasgow and with theft and gambling apparently in their blood. Yet the young priests controlled them effortlessly, although the local shopkeepers did not like their ingrained habits. The young demons 'knocked' everything in sight in the shops of Aboyne – nothing was too big or small for them to steal – and we locals were enthralled by their audacity, having never stolen anything more valuable than the odd apple.

My introduction to algebra at the time was proving rather difficult and my mother even went to the extreme of taking herself off to Aberdeen, some thirty miles distant and into another world from us, to buy a book to solve my blindness. No help at all, but my father, finding pleasant company with these young priests, introduced me to Brother Robert. In one session in his inspired company all the gremlins of algebra were blown away and in the years to come many school prizes blossomed for me from that subject. That tutorial has been as close as I have ever come to experiencing a miracle and my appreciation of those dedicated priests remains to this day.

The gentleness of the faith was also mirrored by the local priest, in whose company one felt a calmness and understanding at odds with the more abrupt attitude of our Episcopalian rector and totally different from the dark, threatening presence of the all-powerful Presbyterian village minister.

Out in the big wide world, my experience of the various faiths has gone through gentle step changes as the power of the churches and their priesthood has eroded. The time when we adopted a respectful attitude, amended our conversation and eradicated our blaspheming in the presence of those in holy orders seems to have passed completely. I feel myself regarding these holy men now with mild amusement at their continuing in a calling which has huge question marks looming over it. Yet I have great admiration for them in giving their lives for the good of mankind, when so many other channels in life were certainly more financially rewarding.

The influence of the Vatican in many Catholic countries sees it dictating policies totally outwith the democratic processes. Its hold over the Republic of Ireland for decades has been massive and it has taken the Irish electorate up until very recent times to see how it has abused its position. In my early days I visited Ireland on a number of occasions before EEC money turned it from poverty to riches. At that time the begging poor were all around you, but the fat priests obviously did not share in only the crumbs of comfort. They also appeared to be at the root of much of the detestation of the UK, as was obvious in our many conversations with them. The sadness of it all was that they appeared really lovely people, but just brain washed to a faith and way of life that they accepted as if destined.

Anyone attending church services and weddings in the Catholic faith cannot but be impressed by the wonderful atmosphere the priesthood can bring to such events. Weddings in particular exude a feeling of happy community spirit which many other faiths often fail to capture. Protestant faiths, on the other hand, appear to believe that removing the glitz brings the message closer to believers. This may have been true in the past, but it does look as if the dazzle of Rome is proving much more attractive to some as our Scottish and English faiths become ever more mundane.

My charitable approach to the problems at present in the Catholic Church is probably not shared by many, but a contrarian opinion is always worth considering. When our purpose is analysed, it is procreation that lies at the root of all continuing life. All our natural bodily mechanisms are geared to this purpose and the male drive to see that it occurs can be a frightening experience. Even average male arousal is difficult to control and accounts for the much talked of date rape, while through the ages the excitement of battle has resulted in mass rape assaults on women when adrenaline levels are grossly elevated.

A religion that demands celibacy as a sign of commitment is hugely ambitious, asking all its priests to ignore their natural drives. If the human brain can succumb to drug addiction after only a couple of episodes of exposure and with many of us unable to control our smoking or eating habits, despite knowing the consequences, then what chance is there of sexual abstinence? I feel fairly certain that few budding priests ever entered a seminary thinking they could not live up to the expectancy of celibacy, but that is to defy nature. Strength of will kept the large proportion fulfilling their vows, but at what cost? Perverted behaviour would have compensated in many and this is where abuse of children occurred.

When many see too much understanding for the criminal and too little for the victim, I realise I am on thin ice here. However, I cannot but think that these priests are also living through their own special hell, sick at heart to be unable to control their basic human weaknesses. I do not condone for one moment their actions, but despite their calling they are active human beings and to deny them their sexual rights is lining up trouble. Priests are recruited from all sorts of backgrounds and I feel certain that many joined their faiths initially as employment, rather than a calling. In England it was expected of the better class families that a son would go to the army and another to the cloth as a matter of course, so to expect a saintly approach from them all is unreasonable.

To the dispassionate observer there does appear an odd logic about much Catholic doctrine. The desirability that their priests should be celibate to show total commitment seems inconsistent with their desire to otherwise encourage human life: no children for their priests, but as many as you like for everyone else. Whether prospective mothers are endangering their own lives or that of the unborn seems of little moment, while to use artificial means to prevent pregnancy is a heinous crime. The quality of life for the young after birth appears unimportant, as long as the foetus is not seen to be murdered in the eyes of many.

To confound us even further we have HIV proven to be partially controlled by the use of contraception, but the Vatican sees nothing illogical about banning such protection and endangering lives. Like an express train driver seeing people on the track but unable to apply his brakes as regulations ban him from stopping between stations. To theologians this may all make sense, but to the outsider it looks like totally selfish, blinkered dogma.

The most startling outcome is that not only does the Vatican get away with such directives from an earlier age, but that its adherents, many of them highly educated and intelligent people, allow this to be perpetuated. A powerful show of independent thought and deed would encourage fresh thinking in Rome.

Is it surprising, therefore, that the Vatican has only paid lip service to the weaknesses of its own foot soldiers over child abuse? It appears to see itself above all other institutions and only grudgingly accepts that it may be associated with some wrong doing. It would far rather solemnly dismiss any misdemeanours as exaggeration by its enemies, who envy its hold over so many followers. Now it is reaping the damning rewards for decades of ignoring and even hiding this problem. It is doubtful that the Vatican has learnt any lesson, however, just as self interest and not wishing to lose face took it two hundred years to allow its adherents to accept that the earth might indeed be circling the sun.

Continuing to ignore the equality of the sexes also has it calling on scriptures from a world of yesterday. Unhappily, many Anglicans are threatening to leave the cosiness of their church over the question of women bishops. To desert an organisation which has the freedom to discuss its difficulties must seriously call into question the quality of such priests. As a Roman Catholic lady perceptively writes to the *Daily Telegraph* – "I am sure I am not the only Catholic who does not welcome a mass influx of misogynists – we have more than enough already".

The abuse scandal, along with other outdated restrictions, should make clear to the world that the Vatican is just another man-made institution with all the usual human strengths and weaknesses. The papal visit to the UK in 2010 was hailed as a great success, with the hope of stimulating fresh interest in the Catholic cause and overcoming the image of a modern-day King Canute.

The Vatican has been a dominant force for so many centuries that any sign of weakness will have huge implications throughout the world and, despite all my criticisms, not necessarily for the better. Just as the United States is losing its world dominance to a burgeoning China, such weakening will bring uncertainty and instability to countries where Catholicism predominates. For the Catholic clergy I have the highest regard; for those in the ivory tower of the Vatican, only frustration and despair.

FAITH – SO WHO CARES OR BENEFITS?

❝FAITH MEANS NOT WANTING TO KNOW WHAT IS TRUE❞

FRIEDRICH NIETZSCHE
19th Century German Philosopher

This final chapter on religious faith looks at the ramblings which have gone before and tries to assess if any of them really matter.

It seems so simple and straightforward when problems are looked at from the fireside of a cosy Scottish glen, but when you get out into the big outside world, life appears much less certain. The rush and bustle of streets crammed with cars, cattle roaming freely and the thunderous noise of 16 million souls inhabiting Delhi and its suburbs, makes all one's ponderings look really unimportant. The thing that unsettles the Humanists amongst us is the level of unfaltering faith. The Hindu religion, now the third most followed in the world, gives one the feeling of spitting in the wind to get anyone to pause long enough to listen to the rational assessment of such beliefs.

Watching the latest World Cup I was amazed at the number of players crossing themselves while coming on to the pitch. The vision of Diego Maradona doing this at least half a dozen times, one after the other, was my lasting memory from that competition. Not that his lord was paying much attention, as the young German team comprehensively knocked his much vaunted Argentineans aside by four goals. The whole world seemed to be calling on religion, or more probably superstition, to carry the day – but for whose selfish benefit?

The problems the Church of England has brought on itself with homosexual clerics and the place of women in the church seems like children fighting over who should be Father Christmas. Life should have moved on. The scriptures filled a void in the past but, like leaving behind ghosts and witches, modern man is entering a phase of civilisation where mysticism will eventually give way to cold logic.

Yet when we point to the ills of strife, hardship and massacres, all down to competing beliefs, we frequently fail to comprehend the benefits. Do the paedophile priests in Ireland totally negate all the good the faith has done for their wider population down through the ages? Through the hardships of poverty, disease and famine, faith has kept many poor people believing in a caring maker who is behind them in their fight for survival – so the benefits here are very clear.

On the other hand, fanaticism over abortion in the USA has seen doctors murdered for simply carrying out their job. Of all the procedures many of us took part in during our training years, abortion, including that for gross deformity, was the most difficult and upsetting for all concerned. This Catholic view of when a foetus is a living being seems unrealistic and those who see abortion as murder make one despair. Thousands die every week in Africa, wars eliminate millions at a time, and even road traffic accidents take a heavy annual toll. Are these anti-abortionists equally worried about such human beings, I wonder?

I do not like abortion, but what I dislike even more is bringing children thoughtlessly into this world under conditions where they are liable to suffer deprivation or abuse. If a child is unwanted, I am far more worried about its possible quality of life and a decision on early abortion should be linked directly to such factors alone and not to some quasi-religious belief. This area of fanatical certainty is not confined to the religious right, but permeates such organisations as the violent animals' rights activists – so who benefits here?

In all parts of the world religions and faith are used as footballs to be kicked around to achieve ends which have nothing to do with love and consideration. In Nigeria, Muslims and Christians slaughter one another, yet no one is a winner. The poor become even poorer and suffering begets suffering, but they are all similar human beings, but with a different 'faith'. The human failings of bigotry, stupidity, ignorance, misplaced loyalties, irrational behaviour – often linked to poverty – all coalesce under the umbrella of religious difference, so wreaking havoc where no one benefits.

What right have we in the affluent West to undermine the beliefs of the millions on the Indian sub-continent and Africa living on the breadline and supported by their faith? Have we atheists the insight into ourselves to go around undermining faiths even in our own country, with nothing to replace it? My real anxiety in a UK setting is that as our own indigenous religions become weaker and spurned, there are powerful religions out there which are nowhere near our advancement in questioning the authenticity of faith.

I have absolutely no racial bias to a multi-ethnic culture in our country, but I have always believed in the old saying, 'When in Rome do as the Romans do'. Different cultures add a new dimension to our society, bringing many strengths. However, I do sincerely believe that excesses, in such as dress, do act as a divisive catalyst and the mosques should be drawing closer to our own institutions to promote greater cohesiveness across the country. We should be calling on the leaders of such communities to put their house in order for the common good of the nation. Government interference will just increase disharmony, but at the end of the day I believe the needs of the majority are paramount.

The siren voice of the extremists who demand repatriation for those who do not conform is too late and now quite unacceptable. Immigrants should, however, from the outset, be left in no doubt that their first duty is to their new homeland. If their religious beliefs and customs come before such commitment and cause friction with their new culture, then they should not have chosen the UK, as they are abusing the very tolerance that attracted them.

Unfortunately it is not only first generation immigrants that bring their potentially alien faiths to the UK, but radicalised second and even third generation Muslims. This has been shown to be a breeding ground for the Islamist militant group Al-Qaeda, first established in 1989 and responsible for the suicide bombing of the London tube station in July 2005. When such faith can attract young men and women to sacrifice their lives for a cause, no matter how ill conceived, then all of us know this is one of the answers to "so who cares?". Also with Iran having 90 percent of its population Shi'a, the most militant branch of Islam, and the state's development of nuclear energy, we must all be concerned.

Designating all those who carry out atrocities as terrorists is equally misleading. Damning your enemy by depicting him as a demon has been recorded since before Roman times and was used extensively by both sides in the World Wars. "War against terror" is also a disingenuous propaganda description for something far more complicated. Like it or not, these terrorists are religious idealists believing fanatically in the right of their cause and prepared to die for it. In other circumstances they may well have been hailed as heroes. If we fail to perceive the basis of their anger, the outcome is inevitably yet more conflict. Unfortunately they are sometimes the fall guys for more subversive elements with a more intricate agenda, only too happy to sacrifice these naïve adherents.

It is also well to consider a definition of fundamentalists; those who know they are right because they have read the truth in a holy book and nothing will budge them. Such fundamentalists and fanatics are present the whole world over and here I may take slight issue with Prof. Dawkins. I sense Dawkins thinks of such people mainly as the result of their religion, whereas I feel these extreme traits have been inherited from way back and if religion had not existed, these characteristics would have been honed to some other cause. Dawkins himself has been described as a fundamentalist atheist, but counters this by describing himself yes, as passionate, but with a scientific approach, prepared to change his ideas if proved wrong. All scientists are not so amenable and have been known to disbelieve fresh proof if it undermines their position.

Whether they are almost the equivalent of religious fundamentalists, or just embittered men who have lost status, must be a matter of conjecture.

On a more positive approach to "who cares" is a European initiative. German autobahns where there is no speed limit have drivers regularly driving for hours at well over a hundred miles an hour. Lorry drivers with a schedule to deliver, salesmen who almost live their lives in their cars, and all those people in a desperate hurry must be under considerable strain to keep their concentration. The opening of churches in rest areas by both Catholic and Protestant churches allows drivers to relax for a short time in prayer or calming contemplation, often with a priest in attendance for those who want to talk. Quiet organ music is another valuable benefit. What do we atheists have to offer to replace this? Does Richard Dawkins ever stop to reflect on the value of such a service, or is he so committed to disproving the dogma of Christianity that he overlooks such trivial benefits?

The Churches of England and Scotland are linked seamlessly into our monarchic system, so little will change even for our next generation. As our intellectuals increasingly find religious concepts irrational, so we as a country will find ourselves, along with other advanced nations, out of step with the world of beliefs. At present we accept everyone's right to worship as they see fit, but when this becomes accepted as mumbo jumbo how will we react and how will those with their faiths react to us?

For the present in the UK, my question of who cares is purely academic and does not appear of imminent importance as believers and non believers appear to live in harmony. Whether this will persist if passive religions are replaced by more militant faiths, or if atheists when in the majority treat faiths groups differently is always open to question.

It is quite bizarre to have TV and radio broadcasts highlighting a world millions of years old, with all the evidence displayed, to be then followed by a religious service extolling the book of Genesis and a world of faith going back just a few thousand years. How can these two portrayals co-exist without the majority of us standing up and saying this is totally absurd?

The problem would appear just too big for the great majority to face up to, so allowing the powerful religions across the world to perpetuate their teachings. This in the medium term will not change, for although the ripple of rational thinking is gradually spreading, there is still no momentum or leadership to challenge the vested interests of such as the Roman Catholic Church. Indeed many religions still play on making atheists appear as devil worshippers, which worked in the past but may not play so easily in the future.

Standing back from my close dissection of this hugely divisive subject, I am filled with a jumble of emotions. A sense of blinkered superiority looking down on these poor deranged followers of a mythology has to be stifled in the knowledge that human beings are intricate and baffling products of their various cultures. The human brain appears to have been capable of doing somersaults, defying logic and not learning from its previous follies.

So we come back to the question, does any of this really matter at this time and to whom? I feel on balance it does with the turmoil caused by vying religions still destabilising the world around us. The Taliban in Afghanistan is held up as a threat to our safety, but how dangerous to the peace of the world is their equivalent in the United States with far more latent power than any small impoverished Asian state? World peace so often appears to hang in the balance with the self interest of nations and their various tribal factions and religious beliefs never far from the surface.

It is worth remembering that despite our different faiths all of us remain human beings, but with varying attitudes and ideas. Out at the fringes are those whom I feel are the extremists who have eschewed all rational argument for or against religion and are impervious to discussion. For the rest of us caught in the middle, we are in our own individual ways trying to make sense of our existence in a changing world.

In Britain today we have entered an age when dividing us all firmly into different camps, religious, agnostic, atheist or just frankly disinterested, is becoming increasingly opaque, with more and more finding themselves in a no-man's land of uncertainty. It is therefore perfectly understandable if many readers adopt that convenient approach of keeping their heads down, only too happy to shrug their shoulders and to let those sleeping dogs slumber.

BY THREE METHODS WE MAY LEARN WISDOM:
FIRST, BY REFLECTION, WHICH IS NOBLEST;
SECOND, BY IMITATION, WHICH IS EASIEST;
AND THIRD BY EXPERIENCE WHICH IS THE
BITTEREST"

CONFUCIUS,
Chinese Philosopher
6th Century BC

BLUE TITS & HOODED CROWS

"HE WHO CAN NO LONGER PAUSE TO
WONDER AND STAND RAPT IN AWE, IS AS
GOOD AS DEAD; HIS EYES ARE CLOSED"

ALBERT EINSTEIN ,
Theoretical Physicist

It is springtime and the bluetits are busily readying the nest box
for the new brood. I have been looking out from my study
window now for 10 years – the time I have taken to write three
books, and wonder at the unfailing return of my little friends
year after year.

I wonder whether they ever think about this never ending treadmill of rearing a brood only to see it disappear by the following year and have to settle down and do the same yet again. I'm simply delighted they keep at it as they are beautiful little fellows but with a sharp will of their own. 'Don't come near this bird table,' seems to be the message to their larger cousins the great tits and 'we are in control here' is the message to those pesky chaffinches. They may be small but these bluetits are cocky and pushy, but I doubt if they know about God watching over them.

Two hooded crows are working their way systematically along the top of my hedge. That blackbird's nest down there somewhere is now in grave danger of being uncovered. I knock loudly on my study window and two wicked black beaks turn towards me for a moment before with a squawk the hooded devils are off. They will be back and nature will once more have run its course. Have crows no Christian feeling for what they are doing, or are they just selfishly fulfilling their own needs? Odd how we can feel so upset about nature in the raw for just across my hedge a herd of cattle browse contentedly, blissfully unaware of their appointment at the slaughterhouse tomorrow morning. Have we a right, as so-called civilised humans, to use other animal life to fulfil our needs, but yet can become so hugely emotional that we are prepared to break the law to stop a hunt chasing one solitary fox?

I can almost understand town dwellers viewing the county

set riding to hounds, after some poor fox, as a barbaric pastime; even as a countryman I have little time for the hunting of stags with packs of hounds. My anger at the spectacle of a stag at bay, exhausted, scarcely able to stand, with tongue hanging out and body heaving with despair, surrounded by baying hounds, is a scene Sir Edwin Landseer, the painter in Queen Victoria's reign, captures intimately. It brings forth for me the despicable thoughtlessness of human nature to put such a fine beast in such a predicament. Somehow the pursuit of the crafty fox does not bring forth similar emotions, which highlights how illogically we cerebrate. Only by stopping to imagine a baying pack of bloodhounds hot on my heels can I replicate the terror of having death breathing down my own neck.

The case for banning fox hunting pales into insignificance compared to some of the other country pastimes, which seem outwith the spectrum of the anti-blood sport lobby. Thousand upon thousand of beautiful pheasants and partridges are reared annually to be blasted out of the skies by civilised man in pursuit of his own pleasure. Our Scottish hills reverberate in August to the sound of gunfire as the very affluent get their pleasure from killing and wounding that master of flight, the red grouse. The banks of our prestigious rivers are lined by fishers awaiting the thrill of a take and the sight of a beautiful silvery salmon leaping skywards in a frantic bid to escape that barbed hook in its jaw. That monarch of the glen may not often be hounded by dogs now, but still falls to pleasure-seeking stalkers with our own royal family often in attendance. At least a well aimed fatal bullet is a thousand times more civilised than chasing a proud animal to ultimate destruction.

I hold up my hand in disgrace that I have partaken of such pleasures through my life, most of all as the young boy intent on catching every little trout in his local burn. Even now I thrill to crumple a towering cock pheasant and have to put up with the shouts of my comrades of it being a pure fluke. Yes, the comradeship, the pleasure of the outdoors, the relaxation from life's tedium all make it so invigorating, but at whose cost?

We blank out the suffering we are causing, we rationalise our battery hens and even *paté de fois gras.* I delight in a very rare sirloin steak, but how would you fancy the mint sauce without a succulent piece of Scotch lamb? How many of us go quietly to church on a Sunday and ask for forgiveness of the Lord for using nature so selfishly to fulfil our own ends? Bad enough trying to justify that we have to feed a world we ourselves over populate. As for abusing nature for pleasure we are totally guilty and by chasing my two crows I am being a blinkered hypocrite.

Spring is really here now and our bluetits are never at peace. I wonder when they are not hatching the latest brood or feeding themselves, how they take up their spare time. They obviously can't play golf or read a book. I supply them with free housing and by the amount of bird seed we buy every week we seem to be keeping them in food as well. No need then to send out the wife to work, so what on earth can they be doing with their time? Do they I wonder suffer from superstitions and keep touching wood hoping that that nasty sparrowhawk or hooded crow hasn't got their number, or are they just happy to be alive? Their life cycle scarcely differs from ours, but it seems they have none of the hassle worrying if their youngsters are getting a good education or if the Stock Exchange is buoyant enough so that they can afford a more salubrious nesting box than I can provide.

The hoodie crows have also reared their latest brood and the parents are intent on teaching them the rudiments of foraging for food. Six are combing the long hedge for my nesting blackbirds and I am enraged at their audacity with me so close to them. A well placed air gun pellet reduces numbers by one and sends out a message that they are not welcome in this garden. However an interesting outcome now shows how even amateur naturalists can learn from observations around them. The previous day the air gun had sent out a similar message to the rabbit colony that was rampaging through my young carrots. Half an hour later, as I went to retrieve the carcase, the brood of crows scatters leaving nothing but a few remnants of fur. Scavenged in an instant, but yet next day the dead crow still lies in the garden undisturbed and remains so three days later when I remove it. Can we take it then that cannibalism is no more acceptable in the crow community than among humans?

Not only are we still in the early stages of unravelling the functions of the human brain, but we may increasingly find that the animal kingdom has even more startling secrets of its own to reveal that will cause us frank amazement.

All very puzzling what this constant cycle of life is achieving for us as well as them. That man pays lip service to a higher being, but lives his life oblivious to his own ungodly ways is disturbing and illogical. Rationalists at least do not require to find excuses in their lives for abusing nature; surely far more honest than the cynicism and double standards practised by so many of the so-called religions.

A little bundle of blue is fluttering animatedly as I draw up at the traffic lights. Struck by an oncoming car the bluetit is thrown into my path to be immediately joined by her mate dashing back and forth from the wall above, in obvious distress. As life drains from the little body I am caught up in the emotion of it all and as the lights change I remain stationary, unable to move as the mini drama plays out. Forced to move with impatient drivers on my tail I still see out of the corner of my eye the little bluetit sitting on the wall, gaze fixed on that fatal spot as cars roll carelessly past. There is something so poignant in this trivial tragedy that for the rest of the day a pall of gloom hangs over me. As a doctor I am used to death and yet I have just witnessed that not only do humans feel sorrow and anguish, but those around us whom we dismiss as too primitive to have similar feelings. This is a salutary experience and those traffic lights remain the headstone to remind me of a touching little episode.

My book is taking longer to compile than I realised and the bluetits are long gone from the nesting box. The squawk of the crow and harsh cry of the magpie still alert me to predators, but apart for the odd robin, a pair of blackbirds and two wood pigeons my garden has been deserted now for weeks. Where have all my little friends disappeared to I wonder? Have they managed to rear most of their brood or have their ever present enemies thinned the ranks. I know from experience, however, that by October and the colder days the odd chaffinch will be sitting on my window sill and the tits will be back in force, clustering around the bird box to remind me it is feeding time once more.

The months march past and nature will soon have completed yet another cycle of life and the routine of the next nesting season will be upon us to make all my little friends one year older. How many of us will pause in the flush of yet another new year and stop to think what this life of ours is all about? We dash hither and thither in constant activity, living our own narrow lives while ignoring much of the natural world around us. Yet with spring leaves bursting from their buds the first notes of bird song will reawaken us to bless our luck to be so fit and well. My friend Geoff, golfing companion for over forty years, will turn to me and with a broad grin say, "Hear the birdies twittering – we must be still alive," and I will give a fulsome reply and inwardly a thousand thanks.

OH, TO BE A DOCTOR

"AIM HIGH IN YOUR CAREER BUT STAY
HUMBLE IN YOUR HEART"

ANCIENT KOREAN ADAGE

He stood well over six feet tall and with his back to our kitchen range in our cramped little living room, he felt like a giant. My mother thought he was wonderful and she would be up at the crack of dawn to see me into fresh pyjamas, don her most becoming dress and make certain the house was spick and span.

Dr Willie radiated professionalism right from his jaunty felt hat, dark suit, collar and tie down to his well polished shoes.

The hint of antiseptic would linger long after he had departed, but it was his reassuring presence that held us in raptures. In those late 1930s only the foul-tasting contents of a medicine bottle covered up the inadequacies of any meaningful treatment, but his bedside manner guaranteed my childhood recovery.

Communities held their doctor foremost in the pecking order and would forgive any diagnostic faux pas or inebriated misdemeanour, as long as he was always smilingly available at all times of the day or night. Along with their total belief in their god, so it was with many of our rural doctors who just could do no wrong. My family was absolutely no different and I grew up in this cosy atmosphere where the medical profession locally, or in that huge city of Aberdeen, were our guardians in adversity.

Did I ever perceive following in the footsteps of the great man is a question I have often asked myself? This goal would have seemed a very distant prospect when attending my two rural schools of Glen Tanar and Aboyne from 1934 until 1944.

My parents never had the opportunity to embrace education, but made certain I did not similarly miss out. My French father had left school around ten years old but by dint of hard work had taught himself English and much more beyond, so that he could hold his own in the employment of the aristocracy. My mother was much more academic, but her formal education ceased at 14 when she took up an apprenticeship as a tailoress. Both in their travels around the world had been convinced that education was the most precious commodity they could bestow upon their son and I was never left in any doubt that a university education was their goal for me.

Few of my rural classmates or their parents ever contemplated school life beyond the earliest leaving age. Perhaps I was fortunate, but Aboyne School that year threw up a number of scholars prepared to move on to higher education and I found myself by one of those freaks of good fortune admitted to Aberdeen Grammar School.

Life is all about developing experience, skills and insight along the way, so what progress in my development came about with an exposure to city life and living away from home? Looking back I was still a very immature young man rooted in my rural upbringing and having only the roughest edges knocked off me with those three years at Grammar. However, to have this experience of schooling in an educational establishment which traced its history back to the 13th century and boasted Lord Byron as its most prestigious pupil, was to have a lasting effect.

Many argue that being given a preferential type of exposure in the premier educational establishment in the region was unfair to the majority. Certainly our Labour town council was to agree and by reducing the status of the Grammar a few years later, along with abolishing the token fees, they reduced it to just another run-of-the-mill district school, so casting aside generations of its heritage in the name of equality.

This typical thinking of the time, to pull everyone down to the same level instead of using imagination and leadership to elevate the deprived upwards, is a lesson still not learned today. Yet as with so much poorly evaluated social engineering, the school continues to flourish academically, so bringing a boom in house values as parents buy their way into its feeder district, thus negating much of the original political purpose.

Imbued in Grammar School pupils was a pride of their start in life, something that was to remain with me through to retirement and beyond, giving me the confidence to feel comfortable at all levels of society. I totally believe in equality of opportunity, but only by improving conditions and not by destroying that which it has taken generations to develop.

The never articulated hope of my parents was fulfilled when in 1947 I entered Aberdeen University to study medicine. Six of my peer group at school, including my best friend, the son of a doctor, had applied for medicine and with no clear idea of what I might do, I just drifted along with them. Not that becoming a doctor ever really filled me with any great enthusiasm. It just seemed to be in the stars after an old gypsy had told my mother when in her teens that she was to have one child, a son who would become either a dentist or a doctor. In retrospect this seems a really fanciful projection to offer to a young miner's daughter, when such outcomes rarely occurred from the working class.

Now it is interesting to listen to so many children from all around the world, many caught up in adversity, who when asked what they would like to be when they grow up opt to be a doctor. This shows that I was a very privileged child just to drift into medicine, and also that in the outside world there are probably thousands upon thousands with this hope at the top of their wish list, but who will never achieve it. University life from a city school background allowed an effortless transition, whereas around me many with more rural backgrounds struggled to find their feet. The early years failed to fire much interest and I made heavy weather of it all before gathering a head of steam towards the end of the course. I was dismayed at the attitude of the University who provided so little assistance to their students who were finding the life so different and difficult. So many of my colleagues fell by the wayside in the early years and although some would say this was necessary to winnow the wheat from the chaff, we lost many valuable students who with a little interest in them would have gone on to be excellent doctors.

Looking back I was a real enthusiast for the things that grabbed me, but in the more mundane I would take only a very superficial interest. Much in my early medical studies fell into this latter category and although it has been my life's work and I have enjoyed much of it, I have never really felt that it truly fulfilled my ambitions.

The years of medical study brought us for the first time into the orbit of the high flyers of the profession in university and the NHS. To the uninitiated eye of the student they were giants and we hung on their words as they formulated not only our education, but our demeanour and attitudes for the years ahead. Some of us may have picked up the odd hint that our gods were not as immortal as they liked us to think, but on the whole we bowed down before them and rarely, if ever, questioned their presentations. We noticed that the more senior they were the more those of lesser stature paid lip service and we quickly sensed that the profession functioned through a distinct order of seniority.

Graduation in 1954, along with many ex-service men, is so long ago that the lessons learnt have probably little relevance to the present day. There was much to be lauded in the course and in the commitment of the lecturers and our student body seemed to be a real cross section of society. In my later years as a university lecturer the medical intakes seemed predominately from the professional classes, with more than 50 percent now women. Also becoming a member of the University Admissions Committee in the 1980s I was disheartened by the attitude of some committee members in not always taking into account the background of some applicants from schools which rarely produced university entrants. Also the attitude of some members to try and recruit only the highest flyers, when it could be argued that many of these would get the least satisfaction from a profession that was, for the majority, more about determined common sense than brilliance.

Doctor in the House with James Robertson Justice playing the irascible chief surgeon Sir Lancelot Sprott was brought to our cinema screens in 1954 at the same time as I entered my first post as a house surgeon in Aberdeen Royal Infirmary. Looking back, I experienced the last of our great characters in medicine – people not dissimilar to Sir Lancelot – who we now recall with nostalgia and not a little awe. Such men, as there were very few women around then, dominated our student years and went on to graft their high standards on to us as young housemen.

My own first chief was Mr Andrew Fowler, a pleasant but slightly aloof surgeon whom we treated as royalty. Having completed his surgical session he would retire to sister's room for a cup of coffee when my fellow resident George McDonald or I would help him on with his coat. We both then dutifully accompanied him downstairs and opened the door of his Bentley for his departure. Watching us from the sister's dining room at our backs was a row of faces and George and I would turn and solemnly bow to them as our chief sedately drove off. All tongue-in-cheek stuff, but that was the ceremony expected towards our chiefs.

Around us then in the Royal Infirmary the nursing staff made sure we appreciated we were at the foot of the pecking order. Nursing sisters dominated our lives, with matron dutifully acknowledged on her frequent visits to see that we young men were not degrading her hospital.

Discipline was strict, cleanliness and order were everywhere expected, while the nurses would not have been out of place on a parade ground. There was not a trolley out of place, not a single obstacle in the corridors and the beds all perfectly in order. Was it all too starched and regimented, I wonder? Certainly the pendulum seems to have swung to the opposite extreme in my experience. Our hospitals have equipment strewn around everywhere, in corridors and wards alike, while the nursing profession appears no longer a smart proud cadre. True the caring is still very evident, but the sense of an immaculate and prestigious profession seems to have sadly disappeared.

The seeds of change were already showing in the 1950s when some of our best ward sisters were seconded into administration. Of all the experts in the field I always felt the ward sisters with their vast clinical experience were the cog in the hospital wheel. Looked up to by all and second only to the consultants in power and prestige, they set the standards of care and efficiency which appears to have been jettisoned in this new age. Although the name 'sister' still exists in our hospitals, this now appears more of an administrative title without the experience and power which kept the wards running like well oiled machines in the past.

The feeling began coming across in my early days that

nursing was as important as medicine and that nurses should no longer be the hand-maidens to a superior profession. Also, there was a subtle change in recruitment, with many well educated young women seeing the expanding associated occupations such as physiotherapy, occupational therapy and radiography as much more attractive.

Nursing has blossomed into having graduate nurses now and the profession's leaders may feel they have done a fine job in hoisting their standing. The harsh facts of life, however, are that despite all the huge advances in treatment and techniques, patients still require the bodily care as in earlier years. There is a nagging sense that washing patients, making beds, or emptying bedpans is just not what a graduate nurse sees as appealing, which may account for the tales of poor care across the NHS. From personal experience, however, many staff continue to be a huge credit to their profession.

Young graduate doctors are, of course, not entrusted with too much responsibility and are required to do two house jobs of six months each before becoming fully accredited to go out into the wide world to practice their trade. A year spent in the Royal Infirmary had certainly prepared me in the best traditions of the profession, both from watching my seniors at work while experiencing the high level of nursing skills.

National Service saw me having the pleasure of relaxing with the Black Watch and the Ghurkhas for the two years in the UK. Nothing measurable was gained from that experience, but the running of my own unit and being responsible for the health of so many soldiers did develop my ability to make decisions without seniors breathing down my neck. Many of my colleagues squirmed over the loss of two years in their climb up the medical ladder, but with no clear thoughts for the future, I just luxuriated in the pleasure of serving Her Majesty.

Hospital practice for a year to take a further degree, and then 32 years in General Practice until 1990 to retire and ponder on whether it had all been worthwhile. Looking back at much of the tedium in General Practice, I still wonder if it would be advisable for some to have a career break into another field, either permanently or for a few years, to revitalise energy and morale.

I was mostly happy in my work, but did I achieve anything of merit and did I fulfil the vocation expected from those who put their trust in me? Another huge area to review was whether the profession itself was due all this respect and trust invested in it by the public, and also how it has responded to being used by the government as a political football.

I have always been dismayed at the idea of competition between our hospitals. I have seen practice competing with practice in my early days and it was a divisive, unhappy experience with few benefits. Evaluating and bringing each hospital to the required standard by rigorous review is surely not beyond the wit of man, while the Conservative/Lib Dem coalition proposal in 2010 to give GPs the billions to direct the service in England seems similarly questionable. GPs are at times barely capable of providing a user-friendly service to patients, without expecting them to become amateur accountants as well. If doctors had wanted to become business men and accountants, surely they would have selected these occupations from the outset. Accountancy has little in common with caring for the sick. Muddled thinking at government level, but it plays well with those ambitious GPs who can see themselves achieving the power and prestige that had evaded their predecessors for so long in the Health Service.

That the shake-up in England will open up the service to private enterprise where the profit motive is dominant is not something I relish. Many GPs, however, may be unable or unwilling to cope with the scale of the responsibility, so will this open the door for private companies to climb aboard to sort out the finances and gradually take over? Also the talk of more patient choice has always had a hollow ring to it. As a GP I strove to provide patients with best advice and choice from my experience over many years, but for patients to carry out their own selection seems a hazardous, unnecessary initiative which I certainly would not advocate for myself.

So what about recruitment into medicine for the future? Do admission committees really understand the personalities required for the different branches of medicine or do they still just tot up the school achievements, scan the admission form and then plump for the highest achievers? Certainly in my time on such a committee, few members had much idea how to evaluate candidates, but this is quite understandable. Thrown now into the pot of confusion is the preponderance of female applicants, so not only are committees trying to define their potential for medicine, but how will they ever fit into the niche where their strengths and lifestyles appear to lie.

These are difficult questions as the profession of medicine is so varied, practised by doctors of differing abilities, who have a broad spectrum of interests and objectives. My impressions of all these factors are assembled from a relatively short period as against medical practice through the ages, but man has not changed much, so it can be surmised that little has altered in human behavioural terms.

A FALLIBLE PROFESSION

**"IN NOTHING DO MEN MORE NEARLY
APPROACH THE GODS THAN IN GIVING
HEALTH TO MEN"**

*CICERO,
Roman Philosopher,
born 106BC*

Dr Willie may have been my childhood hero, but he did have one chink in his armour, although he may well have been oblivious to it. The home visit by the doctor in my youth was of huge importance in our small lives, so when he said he would return on Thursday to check the patient's progress, our whole household waited with bated breath. Hour dragged by, hour after hour; lunch was put off and eventually abandoned until by teatime I was ravenous and my mother was distraught. Next day came and went and it gradually dawned on us that our guardian angel had either forgotten or had just not bothered.

Many weeks later, meeting the bold hero in the village, he remarked I looked extremely well and when asked why he hadn't come back, he airily brushed it aside saying he knew I would stay in bed for another day and by that time have totally recovered. The fact that he had perceived his visit through only his eyes showed an astonishing lack of insight into the doctor- patient relationship and was something I vowed never to do to my own patients when I entered General Practice.

Graduating in medicine for many of us was just the first step in the dark, with little idea which branch of medicine we would eventually follow. It was not until half-way through my own career that I had the scales removed from my eyes by some insightful tutors, and the reality of life fell into place. Only then did I come to realise where my skills and interests really lay and where I should have directed my efforts in the profession.

We are all born with certain strengths and weaknesses, some of us blessed with great talent. The concert pianist, the brilliant actor, the Nobel Prize scientist, the imaginative architect, the world renowned sportsman – the list can go on and on. At a more local level I marvel at the skill of my joiner, or the ability of the computer engineer to sort out a problem in two minutes, when others have wasted hours on it. I note, too, the children around me, often exhibiting those very skills that one or other of their parents are noted for. So has this relevance in deciding which branch of medicine we should follow?

I believe that personality and talent should be blended into the area of work to which we appear most suited. Surgeons are doers, achieving miracles with their ability to absorb and carry out the technical skills to achieve positive results. They require confidence in their abilities and shun too much introspection, so that they can cope with the inevitable ups and downs. They did not, in the past, require much in the sphere of people skills, letting their surgery do the talking. Even today with a greater expectancy of involving patients, their empathy is still considered a bonus.

Hospital physicians, on the other hand, are problem solvers, taking a delight in using their store of medical facts to unravel symptoms and signs and treat accordingly. Their field of medicine, involving the mental as well as the physical requires some insight into the workings of the patient's mind, but this is often seen as a nuisance, interfering with the far more interesting uncovering of some rare physical syndrome.

The field of pathology and other laboratory services has been seen in the past as the territory for those who find dealing with actual patients a bit of a trial. This is unfair on the many gifted doctors in this field, but I often heard the comment that certain undergraduates, appearing to lack an ability to communicate adequately, should consider such a career. This seemed a damning indictment at such an early stage and it was up to us as the educators to highlight and tackle any apparent difficulties.

Psychiatry for me is best characterised by Anthony Clare, late Professor of Psychiatry at Trinity College, Dublin. His programme on Radio 4, *In the Psychiatrist's Chair*, was a revelation and showed this speciality in a totally fresh light. He died prematurely in 2007 at the age of 64, and has been described as perceptive, unafraid and courteous.

Gently psychoanalysing many prominent figures, he uncovered elements about them that were so revealing. Some of those interviewed showed tremendous insight, whereas others we think of as our leaders, left having understood nothing. Clare's whole persona breathed someone committed to not only mental illness, but also to human nature.

An interest in the human mind, both the normal and the disturbed, should be the recruiting ground among our graduates for this speciality, but a number of factors appear to negate all this. There is a sense that psychiatry is the Cinderella of the NHS, inadequately resourced and prioritised, it has suffered from a poor, unglamorous image even within the profession itself. In my time I could detect no distinct type of personality that could be defined as the average psychiatrist. Some were physicians who had left what appeared to be their true niche to enter psychiatry, but continued to act like physicians. Many were excellent people, but for me totally in the wrong occupation. The difficulty in recruitment meant at times a faster route to becoming a consultant, which must have had its attractions. Then there were doctors who it was hard to fit comfortably into any particular category, and who must have just drifted in, as they were even difficult for me to relate to, never mind disturbed patients.

Then we come to the general practitioners. The ideal GP should be all things to all men, in fact to have a multiplicity of skills to deal with the whole gambit of health as well as an interest in human living. It has been said that general practice is really an art form with only an overlay of science. However, the vocational sense to treat all illness in a family and social setting in which he/she is totally conversant, should be the vision, unaffected by whether patients are rich or poor. That this ideal is beyond most of us is understandable, but should still be a goal to reach out for.

As in psychiatry, however, the reality can be so very different. General Practice over the decades of the NHS has suffered from being the poor relation of the profession. In the past it was something failed specialists fell back into, as well as the lower half of any medical year, who saw it as the easiest option for a livelihood. This observation is understandably hugely upsetting for those who genuinely opted for family medicine and as such it is being tackled resolutely by the Royal College of General Practitioners, but it is an unhappy legacy from years gone by. Even before the NHS, general practice contained a variety of personalities, many with the unenviable reputation of having taken 10 years to graduate, while others just fell all too easily into father's footsteps.

The NHS established in 1947 had been in existence for 11 years before I experienced it as a doctor in the community. The years before the war had seen GPs battling to hold together their livelihoods in a competitive environment, when ethical behaviour was quite frequently breached. Having been fully compensated by government for their private practices at the inception of the health service, such behaviour should have lessened.

Doctors, however, used to holding on to as many patients as possible, were slow to change, even being prepared to keep on patients tens of miles away from their practice area. Any neighbouring practice getting a mention in the media or any positive publicity was immediately jumped on and reported to the local disciplinary committee, or the General Medical Council in serious cases. A patient recommending a doctor could also land that doctor in trouble, although he had played no part in the process, but was still held to be advertising. Doctor watched doctor and practice watched practice, which I found a distasteful way to conduct our affairs.

Some doctors in these circumstances proved to be less than pleasant, while others treated their juniors and assistants with little consideration. Senior practitioners in the past had often been treated harshly, both financially and with a heavy workload by their seniors, but many instead of learning from this experience passed on the same conditions to their juniors. Advising one of my close colleagues to beware the doctor he had agreed to join with a view to partnership, as he was the umpteenth assistant to have such an offer, I found myself threatened with legal action when my advice leaked out. This type of bullying made us very aware who was in control and we became very careful what we said and to whom.

My own early days in practice were marred by a cut-throat rivalry between our two local practices in neighbouring villages. The pros and cons of who was right or wrong have never been properly evaluated, but both sides were probably at fault. My senior partner had set up a branch surgery opposite the house of the doctor in the neighbouring village in retaliation for what he saw as an unfair inheritance of a practice he thought was to join up with him. In all the years while my senior was alive, he passed fewer than half a dozen words with his neighbour and there was always an undercurrent of animosity between the practices. Patients were at times caught in the crossfire and I always thought this pettiness was a poor reflection on a proud profession.

Gradually maturing in this atmosphere, I began to kick against the traces of a life controlled by a small cabal of seniors in the district. Gradually in time, we as the younger members came to undermine and eventually replace them with a system that fully recognised the individual's place. Although there were many doctors of huge integrity at that time, there were others who loved the power and were ably abetted by yes-men who undermined my belief for the future that doctors were a profession to be trusted implicitly.

So what has changed since Dr Willie warmed his posterior against our kitchen range all those distant years ago? General Practice in my early years was still a cottage industry, with city practices often working out of dingy little side shops, or affluent practices out of the dining room of a large house with the maid tidying up after the last patient left. Family medicine has certainly modernised and GPs are now mostly housed in prestigious premises with a plethora of staff and ancillary services attached. On the other hand, doctors have lost much prestige, if only because it appears that it requires half a dozen to do what one god-like figure did in the past.

Critics bemoan the loss of that paternalistic figure of old, while doctors appear in danger of relegating themselves to secondary in importance to their practice nurses, who take on an ever greater role at a fraction of the cost of a GP, causing ripples of dissatisfaction among some. Meanwhile a box-ticking culture has been forced on the profession who attempt to cover the whole population rather the minority who in the past attended only when frank illnesses occurred. A progressive, well-intentioned goal, so those of us in old age who bemoan the lack of personal care must weigh up the pros and cons very carefully.

The National Health Service has been hailed as the blueprint for medical care across the world, but over the years has become tarnished. One of the more disgraceful images of the profession occurred at its inception when Aneurin Bevan, in 1948, the architect of the NHS, did a deal with the Royal College of Physicians to allow members to work in the new service, while still keeping their lucrative private practices – ever after known as the agreement reached by "stuffing their mouths with gold".

Since then consecutive governments have tampered with the NHS organisation, with too many mediocre outcomes and little insight, all at great expense.

The concept of General Practice as a business within the NHS, contracted to a monopoly employer, namely the government, has always pulled doctors in different directions. By dividing their attention from giving a 100 percent to patient care, they sacrifice valuable time in running their practices on commercial lines. This branch of medicine is not for the starry-eyed, as the work becomes hugely mundane after a relatively short period. Then it becomes a question of dogged tenacity to keep standards up, or finding something to compensate for those hours of endurance, dealing with constant patient expectancy.

In the past, many senior doctors were to be found on the

golf course, while their juniors did the chores. Others selected their work to tend only those in the congenial West End, leaving the juniors to cope with the housing estates. I hold up my hand guiltily and accept that I used my half days and more in the committee work of running the NHS and the BMA, but as a diversion it probably still ranks on a par with being on the golf course.

In our hospitals, the days of a recognised chief with power in a ward has disappeared, with administrators now appearing to wag the dog. Specialisation perhaps sees adequate treatment for one problem, but when a number of different problems occur together, there appears to be no-one taking overall responsibly. Tales of excellent hospital treatments are balanced out by those of the totally inadequate. There is a lack of leadership among our senior consultants, who appear to shrug their shoulders and leave it to those who are only interested in targets and statistics. In an era when medicine is moving on apace in its interventions, blending the service into a cohesive machine is undoubtedly difficult, but there is no excuse for poor professional care from either the medical or nursing professions.

Through the years I came to rate both my fellow GPs and hospital colleagues on the basis of not only their standard of care, but also how they qualified as human beings. I learnt to ignore the brusque sarcastic surgeon, while still referring all my patients to him in the knowledge that he was the best available.

On the other hand, the casual, pleasant physician was quickly ditched as my patient's continuity of care demanded a totally focused approach. Many doctors were excellent, but more than a few exhibited a side that was all about themselves, giving little thought to those around them.

The practice of medicine is a truly honourable profession and demands the very highest standards from its practitioners. We have, of course, had the black sheep such as Dr Bodkin Adams, a GP in Eastbourne who was found guilty as a fraudster, but never convicted of murder. It was never established whether to gain from his rich patients' deaths he was simply applying euthanasia, but the fact remains that in the years from 1946 to 1956, 160 of his patients died under suspicious circumstances, 132 of these having left him money or valuables.

Similarly, Dr Harold Shipman who practised as a GP in Hyde in Cheshire was found guilty of murder in January 2000. It was discovered that he had committed 218 murders, but many more may have gone undetected. Described as a serial killer, he even managed to kill while awaiting trial. He hanged himself in prison in January 2004, but huge questions still hang over how he got away with killing such numbers for so long. His fellow doctors in the district were signing his cremation forms as being satisfied with the details of the deaths. Not until a funeral director brought it to the attention of a lady doctor did anyone begin to suspect – an appalling tragedy with the implications going far beyond Shipman.

Changes in life are often like the pendulum of a grandfather clock, swinging from one extreme to the next and only momentarily passing through the mid point. The consultation of yesteryear was little more than a veterinary exercise with patient input minimal and the outcome usually up to nature to heal. From the 1960s onwards a core of enthusiasts changed all this into a sophisticated encounter when every nuance of patient behaviour was noted before reaching a diagnosis. Then with a battery of highly potent drugs, of which many of us had only the barest of knowledge, the patients had a wand waved over them and health was hopefully restored.

Making professions more sophisticated does have some drawbacks. The nursing profession having introduced an academic qualification into training, the perceptions of its new recruits imperceptibly changed. Nurses are seen as equals to doctors, but with complimentary skills, so it is understandable if washing incontinent patients or emptying bedpans has become less appealing. Similarly with doctors' training – is there a danger when introducing complicated skills too soon of losing focus and ignoring the salient problems while unearthing the adjuncts?

During my career I realised that the patient might want much more than a cure for his sore throat. Small clues could unearth far greater worries which the patient found difficulty in articulating. This was excellent educationally, but it is a difficult balance to get right. I have sensed in recent times some young doctors becoming confused and appearing more interested in the unsaid than the complaint itself. With the intrusive computer interfering with eye contact and the need to review routine checks-ups, the outcome of such consultations can feel almost as unsatisfactory as the opposite extremes of days gone by.

Those of us who have required the assistance of the NHS, however, are in no doubt of its huge benefits. My wife battled with terminal cancer for 10 months, undergoing chemotherapy and extensive surgery on two occasions. The system worked almost perfectly, providing a service of unbelievable commitment which could not have been bettered if I had been in the USA and spent the best part of a hundred thousand dollars. Those of us who criticise parts of our health service do not do so for negative reasons, but to try to improve this wonderful concept of free health care for all.

Dr Willie died blissfully unaware that despite all his huge strengths it was his Achilles heel of personal unawareness that would have the greatest influence on my career. Seventy years later the lesson of his lack of perception is mirrored in today's doctors by their obsession with the ancient stethoscope. Some, with nowhere to stow the stethoscope appear relaxed to dangle such an unhygienic instrument around their necks, while newly qualified doctors in their first house jobs can be excused for showing off their L-plates with some bravado. Otherwise it is a surprising failure to appreciate that using such a rudimentary instrument as a badge of office tells the intuitive so much about us.

With American and UK television soaps and advertising glorying in depicting doctors and their handmaidens decked out in this basic tool, someone should have the insight to see how such imagery trivialises the profession. It is bizarre that a profession taught to have understanding of human nature should fall so naively into such unthinking lemming-like showmanship. I can almost hear the growl of displeasure from my past chiefs if any junior had dared flaunt his status in such an unseemly manner.

Introspection is viewed by many as a weakness and none more so than in the medical profession. Yet it is this so-called weakness that allows us not only to understand ourselves, but also allows us to amend our actions towards others. Even today with far more sensitivity towards the feelings of others, too many doctors and nurses still appear unable to climb into the patient's and relative's shoes, especially those of the elderly.

Having now been retired for an unbelievable twenty years, I view our modern NHS with a degree of anxiety and the possibility of hospital admission as a real hazard. All generations appear to think that their times had the highest standards and perhaps I fall into this trap. Old age, however, allows a totally different perspective from when your career lay ahead of you. Now I have experienced life from both sides of the fence and although our medical profession is rightly regarded as a national treasure, it has still some considerable way to go to educate its workforce to gain the telling insights to make it worthy of its enviable public reputation.

Women, their Rights and Medicine

"Nobody will ever win the Battle of the Sexes. There's just too much fraternising with the enemy"

Henry Kissinger,
born 1923,
German born American politician, diplomat
and Nobel Peace Prize recipient

Although I am not quite old enough to remember the doings of the Suffragettes, their fight for recognition makes for exciting reading. Women's suffrage in the United Kingdom as a national movement only became really established around 1872. The real drama began in1903 when a lawyer, Mrs Emmeline Pankhurst, along with her daughters, set up The Women's Social & Political Union in Manchester. They recruited many firebrands to their cause, probably the most notable and remembered being Emily Davison.

Civil disobedience was their principal method of confrontation before World War I of 1914, when Emily Davison was involved in smashing windows, secreting herself away in the House of Commons and along with others, chaining herself to the Downing Street railings outside No 10. They set fire to post boxes, threw stones and even produced primitive bombs, while supporters sent to prison often went on hunger strike. Emily Davison used the hunger strike to get her early release on occasions, as the Government was fearful that the bad publicity of a woman dying in prison could only strengthen their cause.

Emily Davison was born in 1872 and despite having a difficult financial upbringing, she graduated from London University with a first-class honours degree in English Language & Literature and became a teacher. She gained immortality on 4 June 1913 when at the mature age of 40 she dashed from the crowd watching the Epsom Derby and threw herself in front of the King's horse, Anmer. Receiving fatal injuries, she has become a talisman in the subsequent fight for women's equality, which was finally achieved in 1928 when women gained equal voting rights with men.

Like all such rights, winning them was just the beginning of the story rather than the end. Over the decades, even into the 21st century, women have had to fight at all levels of society. In many occupations, women continue to be paid at a lower rate than men doing exactly the same work. Talk in business of women still finding it difficult to break through the glass ceiling to take over the highest jobs in the land, rankles with many.

My own memories from childhood were of the woman's place being at home to look after the children and run the household, while the husband earned the livelihood. To have young children and to have even a part-time job was frowned upon, while in most occupations marriage meant a girl giving up her job. This was accepted as the norm; my own mother would never have dreamt of taking up any sort of outside occupation while I was growing up.

Throughout my education, lady teachers played a major role. My lower schooling was totally in the hands of the ladies and I remember them all with a degree of affection and a massive amount of awe and appreciation. The name of Miss Kate Pirie at Glentanar School in my infant years brings back memories of the ruler across the fingers of the left hand and exasperation at my colour-blind raffia work with browns, greens and reds all mixed together. The repetitive chanting of c–a–t and m–a–t along with our multiplication tables remains with me even today. The memory abides with me of the elation of doing something worthwhile in her eyes to allow me to choose a book from her cupboard, or the cosiness of clustering around the little fire with her on cold bleak snowy days to do our lessons.

The move to Aboyne School and into the gentle reassuring presence of Miss Reid settled me down from being an anxious, stressed little boy, until the next year and into the class of Miss Thrasher Milne. Miss Milne was back to the Miss Pirie type of teaching of stress and achievement, but by now I was much better prepared and her personal interest in my progress, I believe, laid the basis for me eventually reaching university. A rather aimless qualifying year under Miss Clubb and I was in upper school and again into the presence of the ladies – the best remembered being Miss Beinge. She struggled to get me to pass my Latin, but I surprised her and myself by passing French more handsomely than anticipated.

On to the Aberdeen Grammar School where the upper school emanated a male-dominated environment in keeping with centuries of tradition, although I did have a lady French teacher who sadly did little for my antipathy for all things French. Looking back, my later education was dictated in a strong male atmosphere, but in the early stages it was the women who really moulded me.

Through my medical university years women played very little part and only the looming presence of the nursing profession in our later years of training made us realise the influence of another powerful group. My year as a young houseman in Aberdeen Royal Infirmary was the first time I had come to realise the true importance of a profession almost totally composed of women. From matron down through the nursing sisters to the staff and training nurses, I became a total fan of this wonderful group of people. In truth they were often more impressive than my own profession, which I was beginning to view as an insider and realising it was not all that it appeared to the public.

In my medical year of 1954 there were 94 students, only 25 percent of whom were women. Even more staggering were the figures for our teachers throughout our undergraduate years. We were exposed to the teachings of four women and 84 men – almost unbelievable in this day and age, but indicative of not only the level of recruitment to the profession, especially from the years before World War II, but also the paucity of openings for women doctors in hospital and university. With modern medical intakes to our universities now regularly recruiting around 60 percent of women, the whole scene has radically changed.

Out into my career, leaving hospital practice behind and entering general practice I became a partner in a husband and wife set-up which allowed me a fine insight into how part-time women fitted with difficulty into such a life. At that time the gradually increasing intake of women into medicine was feeding not only into general practice, but also into the very important public health sector. Here it was noticeable that the Medical Officers of Health and most of their deputies were male, while the run of the mill duties were being carried out by the female medical staff.

It always struck me that the pioneering ladies in General Practice were a really tough breed, having to exist in what was a male dominated sector of the profession. I developed a high regard, not only for their dedication and high standards, but for their ability to disregard the undertones of hostility from their male colleagues. Under-represented at all levels, both locally and nationally, they brought forth many outstanding personalities such as Mary Esslemont and Joan Burrell in Aberdeen, fit to compete with the most big-headed alpha males.

General Practice was dominated by the senior male members of the profession who saw their standing as unassailable. Feted by the general public as the backbone of communities, especially in country districts, they frequently viewed themselves as the crème de la crème of their area. They themselves had probably come up the hard way by being assistants to previous god-like figures and when they reached their own exalted positions, they carried on as had their predecessors.

The end of the war followed by the introduction of the National Health Service in 1947 changed the dynamics of the process. No longer were the GP principals the owners of their practices; they were now beholden by regulation to run their practices for the common good, while all fee-paying by non private patients was abolished.

Women were still regarded as little more than handmaidens to their dominant male colleagues. Having become involved in not only medical politics but also getting elected to the advisory side of the NHS, I began to realise how strong the antipathy was to giving women more power. I saw at first hand how committees made up totally of men used the regulations to deny my own female partner her full rights, while my attempts to get one or two women elected on to our committees was stamped on by my powerful seniors.

Continuing on the advisory committees up until my retirement in 1990, we had no female representation on those areas of power, while even in the university Department of General Practice no female lecturer had been recruited. I presume, in these days when the influence of women in General Practice has become so obvious, that all this is history.

With the increasing level of female medical graduates emerging through the decades, it became obvious that the tectonic plates of UK medicine were really shifting. I was often scoffed at by colleagues back in the 1970s for my prediction that General Practice would become a women-dominated branch of medicine by the early 21st century. It seemed obvious, with public health having faded into obscurity and with many hospital specialities not geared to accept other than full-time staff, that General Practice was the only branch to absorb them adequately.

Over the years I had well over 20 young trainee GPs attached to my practice and a countless number of final-year students. More and more often these trainees and students were young women. I developed a huge regard for the majority – all highly intelligent, interested to learn and above all, stimulating people to have around. I came to regard many as nothing less than my own daughters and I revelled in doing my utmost for them.

Having fought so hard to promote women's points of view in the highest quarters, it would seem that now I should be satisfied with this influx of high calibre women and their rights being at last taken seriously. However, as so much in life never quite lives up to your hopes, so this tidal wave of female graduates was bringing it own problems into an area I viewed as the centre piece of good practice.

For me, the bedrock of family general practice through the ages has been the wonderful ability to give personal care to patients, developed over years of treating them and their relatives, while getting to know all their in-built problems and foibles. The continuing personal care of the house-bound and the ability to give patients the feeling that in ill health and in their enfeebled years they had their friendly family doctor there to depend on, was a service of tremendous significance. Despite the increased demands that came with the NHS, many of us continued with this concept, which made the less attractive aspects of the work seem so much less tedious.

Just before I retired in 1990 all this began to change, with home visiting and dropping in to see the house-bound being seen as not time-efficient; the profession seemed to be more and more driven by financial incentives rather than doing a good job for its own sake. Why do bankers require a bonus culture to achieve success for themselves and their employees? Similarly what has happened to our medical profession when money comes before vocation? I blame the Government and the Civil Service for being oblivious to the fact that teachers, nurses and doctors had a tradition of service to their communities which has now been cast aside by ignorant insensitivity and this wonderful tradition has been almost lost forever. The medical profession, however, is not clear of blame as our own leaders often appear more focused on power, politics and remuneration than vocation and duty.

So where does all this fit in with women's rights? Recognition of academic ability and equality of opportunity has led to a surge of entry into the prestigious professions of law and medicine by young women. Does this fit into the needs of society or have they been ignored as rights become the buzzword? The marked increase in the legal profession of full-time and part-time female lawyers is evident and although I find it irritating to being regularly told my lawyer only works Monday and Thursday or is off on maternity leave, this does not have any far-reaching consequences for me. In medicine, however, I believe it has much greater implications, particularly in General Practice where part-timers especially cannot be expected to fit into the concept of continuing personal care.

Practice management argues that the ability to use the available work force as required takes precedence over a personal doctor service, which a large proportion of patients probably fail to value in any case. For the perceptive and distressed patient, of course, the loss can be huge as having no one responsible to see a disease process right through often brings about the worst of outcomes, with no one doctor seeing the patient's welfare as their particular responsibility.

Even in my time American mothers frequently complained that their problem with the NHS was a failure to determine who had overall supervision for, say, their child's illness, which frequently saw them shuttled from doctor to doctor with apparent haphazard changes of treatment and little or no follow up. This, they maintained, was in marked contrast with their own medical service in the USA. Nothing much appears to have changed as recently a family member saw three different part-time lady doctors over a 12-day period, being given three different powerful antibiotics all for a minor ailment, despite valiantly trying to be seen by the original doctor.

This whole area raises moral and ethical questions and is guaranteed to raise the hackles of this new generation of professional women who see it as a hard fought right to reach their ceilings of achievement equally with men. I thoroughly appreciate their point of view, but it does raise the question of whether the individual or society is the most important?

The talents of women professionals are at least on a par with their male counterparts, a fact that has never been in doubt, but whether they in their particular circumstances can always bring the commitment to the job, when married and/or with young family, is a debatable point. Whether it is fair on themselves, their family, the practice or patients seems often lost in the declaration of their rights. The attraction of living on two salaries and keeping up with the lifestyle of their peers, while providing such extras as private schooling may also play a subliminal part.

The counterbalancing argument is that there is a tremendous demand by patients to be seen by a lady doctor and many are quite prepared to wait until they are available.

With our hospitals staffed with so many foreign-born graduates and with some specialities totally taken over by them, why if we are turning out hundreds of our own doctors every year, do we have to depend on so many outsiders? An advanced Western democracy has got something wrong to rob the poor countries of their scarce resources to keep our institutions functioning under such circumstances. Is the suffering and poverty in so many third world countries of a lesser concern to us than upsetting an already privileged section of our own population?

If, for instance, our police force recruited by quality alone, it could end up with over a 60 percent female intake. Fine in the days of tranquillity, but what happens when we have riots, angry demonstrations or other duties requiring male muscle. Not a satisfactory way then to recruit our police force or our Armed Forces, so surely women's rights must be balanced by the needs of their occupations. Educating doctors, which costs at least £250,000, and then being unable to use a high proportion because of totally foreseeable drawbacks, while importing foreigners to do what we should be able to do ourselves, appears to be economic nonsense.

As a father, I seriously worried about my son achieving the skills to maintain himself at the standard of life he had been accustomed to. With my daughter, I was much more relaxed and was quite happy to fund her to two different degrees, while she found her feet. As she was attractive, vivacious and intelligent I was indulgent, knowing that marriage and family would follow in due course. I was proud of her achievements in preparing herself for a worthwhile life which she might choose to follow in addition to her responsibilities as a mother. Subsequently, able to work flexi-hours, she has brought up two children, apparently effortlessly and with a level of mothering my own mother would have thoroughly approved of, while fulfilling her professional ambition in life.

Many of my own women trainees were in exactly my daughter's situation, having achieved from educated middle class backgrounds, with proud parents and the girls themselves seeing their medicine as much as an interesting hobby as a vocation. They probably sensed, but never admitted, that they had achieved a second string to their bow, but that their real fulfilment would probably be family life with children.

In our daily lives we are fixated on education, occupation, leisure, material possession and the pursuit of happiness, while almost totally ignoring why we are all here in the first place.

Modern working practices can undoubtedly be tailored towards individual needs and women can often fulfil their obligations all round satisfactorily. Whether the past ideals of General Practice can ever be blended in with women's rights and men with only a partial commitment, however, looks increasingly forlorn. All, sadly, in the name of progress.

Christina Odone in her book *What Women Want,* points out how the working-class mother is forced to take up part-time work just to make ends meet, with a husband in a poorly paid job and a couple of infants. How the stress of it all at times becomes almost too much for her, when all she wants is to have more time to give to caring for her children. Set against this are "the cosy careerists' club that for too long has monopolised the public debate on what women want. This tiny elite, devoted to their high-flying remunerative careers, are totally unrepresentative of ordinary women". She goes on to compare this group, able to afford carers and nurseries, while preaching about their rights, as against those women who cherish their interdependence within couples. Another telling line is "they rate career above caring and believe that self-realisation comes only through professional success".

All this may be very sweeping as I know many of these women and they are a great credit to the profession, but I come from a different generation of oldies. I look back with great appreciation to the reassuring benefit of a mother always being on the doorstep to welcome me home from school, while I believe there is increasing evidence to suggest that mothers bonding with their children goes on far longer than originally perceived.

Finally, a year or two ago I noticed that a local practice had three partners all off on maternity leave together. True, without the full facts it is unfair to draw too many conclusions, but where was the consideration, not only to the smooth running of a practice as a business, but even more the duty of care to the patients who provided those doctors' livelihoods. One off on leave is probably inevitable under present day arrangements; two looks like bad planning, while three is, if not abuse, certainly misuse of their rights. Have rights blotted out the realisation that all of us, both men and women, are here to mould ourselves into society and not expect society to conform to us.

If any GP can be replaced with a stand-in at any time we have really thrown away the jewel in the crown of past practice. If personalised family medicine is to be reduced to a faceless public health service, then surely a salaried service staffed by full- and part-time doctors on a rota would be able to use all those with varying commitments and be paid simply by session and experience. Practicing from large multidiscipline clinics, many doctors would be released to practice medicine instead of being involved in time-consuming business practice administration for which they have no training. This very sadly seems the logical answer to the modern trend of practice instead of our present halfway house with a multitude of practices and premises duplicating one another, while costing the state an ever increasing fortune to finance. All very disappointing.

I do not think those running our affairs, whether men or women, really appreciate what it means, especially to older intelligent members of society, to have the tremendous reassurance of having someone they can relate to personally, whether in medicine, dentistry, banking or law. Such a service in many spheres has been discarded as being of too little importance, or not economically justifiable. Only when those in power reach retirement will they realise what has been lost, but all too late by then.

I am hugely indebted during my life to women in many walks of life and have over the years done my best to further their cause. It would therefore be hugely disappointing if, when they have almost reached equality of rights with their male counterparts, that some should adopt those very attitudes that they so detested in men throughout their years of struggle.

THE CONUNDRUM OF OBESITY

"THE DEVIL HAS PUT A PENALTY ON ALL THINGS WE ENJOY IN LIFE. EITHER WE SUFFER IN HEALTH OR WE SUFFER IN SOUL OR WE GET FAT"

ALBERT EINSTEIN

Disfiguring obesity first struck me on a wonderful trip through the Canadian Rockies out to the Pacific coast in the 1980s. The further we penetrated into the backwoods of Canada the more obvious it all became. Lovely rural people in these small townships and hamlets, but bedevilled by a condition that over the next twenty years would grow to epidemic proportions. I had always imagined backwoods Canadian men to be of lumberjack proportions and in this I was not mistaken, but it was their womanfolk who left the greatest impression. Dressed in shell suits and of gross size was how they appeared to live, wearing the same shapeless garments whether in daily work or eating out in the evening. Having always admired a shapely, well-dressed female form, I found the experience very depressing and it was not until we returned to Calgary that an elegant passer by reminded me that not all North Americans had left chic culture behind.

Travelling in the United States on later occasions cemented this image firmly in my mind, as male and female fellow travellers alike could take up two seats in bus, train or airliner. Now the affliction has spread into our own domain and everywhere you look in the UK the human frame has been distorted with this disfiguring condition.

Diet and the increasing use of motor transport instead of exercise would have accounted for my Canadian experience. Out in the wilds no one would be bothered about their appearance and with no peer group to shame them, drifting into obesity was perfectly understandable. Jumping into their huge gas guzzlers to cover a few hundred yards seemed the norm, so no wonder the body had stopped burning up energy and instead had resorted to building up layers of fat.

The years of war from 1939 saw our diets severely restricted, but it seemed to do none of us much harm and obesity seemed only to occur in those genetically predisposed to it. A poor working wage was also a constraint to over-eating on fancy cakes etc., but such little treats are well remembered. Smoking was almost universal among the men, with many ladies not far behind. The threat of cancer and the social stigma that has become attached to it has relegated smokers into a perceived underclass, but now to be possibly replaced by those afflicted by gross fatness. Meanwhile, alcohol abuse in Scotland shows little sign of abating, although the minimum pricing debate is at least a promising innovation for a weakness that has almost become a proud national tradition.

From general observation in the UK, obesity appears to be reaching worrying levels not only in adults, but increasingly among the young. It is something which cannot simply be tackled by diet alone without looking more closely into psychological factors as well as lifestyles. The inherent dangers, especially for our grandchildren, are so great, however, with a huge increase in diabetes and its complications that it requires much thought and far greater effort to counteract.

Looking at the problem from a purely superficial level, obesity is simply taking in more fuel than is being used up, so resulting in layers of adipose tissue. The answer is straightforward; by restoring the balance between the two the problem is solved. For a large proportion of the middle class this appears to be the case, apart from those predisposed to obesity. In others, especially the less affluent, the battle of the bulge appears increasingly lost, the initiatives to counteract it increasingly useless.

If the problem appears related to class, what differences do we perceive that could be brought to bear for a more general solution? Looking at the successful campaign over smoking, what lessons have we learned? First and foremost I feel the soundly based propaganda campaign left no doubt in intelligent minds of the hazards individuals faced if they continued to smoke. This rapidly became linked to peer group disapproval of those continuing to smoke, with the middle classes highly sensitive to such pressure. Those most habituated to nicotine found difficulty stopping, but the greatest proportion ceased, so that it has become unusual to be in the company of smokers. A smoker who continues with this habit is now viewed with a certain level of amusement, even condescension, which ensures that he/she has to be fairly thick skinned to ignore the atmosphere.

This level of society that has ostracised smoking appears to be made up of the professions and business sectors and involve the more affluent members of society. From the evidence outside city offices, hospitals and other establishments, the message has had much less effect. I put this down to the fact that group pressure among these smokers is either not present or so feeble as not to affect their smoking behaviour at all.

Coming from a working-class background, I am extremely

uncomfortable defining levels of behaviour and practices down to the UK's unfortunate class structure. However, there is little doubt in my experience that the lower the social class, the more you come across health and socially related problems. This should be self evident as the less well paid jobs or those unable to hold down jobs are the most vulnerable to poverty and to eating the cheapest foods. However, such is anxiety not to offend, that we hate to be seen as being judgemental, when we cannot progress without identifying the underlying reasons.

For those of us who are tall and slim it is all too easy to criticise those who are continually fighting the flab. The well known past argument of what type of fat we have between those with brown or those with white fat appears to have been overtaken by dividing us into three basic types. The ectomorph is the skinny type with a super-fast metabolism, but which makes it difficult to gain weight or build up muscle. Then there is the endomorph with a fat body, big bones and a rounded shape which puts on weight and muscle all too easily. The final type is the mesomorph who is in between in ability to put on muscle, while still managing to lose fat like an ectomorph. Unfortunately all shapes are down to genetics, so interchanging for the best is outwith science at present; we have to deal with our body shapes as best we can. In the obesity epidemic this centres mainly on the endomorphs, although the indolent in the other groups can also be implicated.

Methods of assessing an individual's target weight have been sophisticated over the years and the Body Mass Index (BMI) which measures height against weight for the different sexes is the present gold standard. The internet provides a simple ready reckoner for carrying out this calculation, which can also incorporate age for greater accuracy. Grades vary from underweight, normal, overweight to obese. Men are considered borderline at 25 percent body fat and clinically obese at 30 percent, while women are borderline at 30 percent and clinically obese at 35 percent body fat.

Understanding where we fit in to this outline is the key to tackling the problem of suspected excess weight, but it needs a level of intelligence, interest and commitment to have any hope of achieving our goals. I feel we are tackling the obesity epidemic with one hand tied behind our backs. Smoking was a habit practiced across the whole spectrum of society, so when it was shown to be potentially fatal there was enough momentum in that message alone to make the sensible think seriously about the implications. The propaganda campaign could be brought to bear on all levels of society without stigmatising any particular group. Only now with the fight almost won among a large section of the community is there a sense that an underclass of citizens continues to smoke. Getting them to stop may well defy any message or frightening evidence, as they are either so addicted or are those who live for today and never bother thinking of tomorrow.

The battle of the bulge provides a totally different problem as it is levelled at a specific group of people, many of whom are already at the foot of the social scale. Right away it can be seen in class terms, with those at the top so aware of the dangers that they bring direct and indirect pressure on their own social group to adopt a healthier style of living.

Among my colleagues I am very conscious of the disapproving glances at those in our immediate group who tend to be overweight and the message comes loud and clear and is no different to that from the smoking lobby. The additional factor that our children could be affected carries even greater responsibility and ensures our diligence. Not that I think the fight is won even here and the message must be continuously reinforced for those who are tempted to slip backwards.

Lower down the social order, however, things appear very bleak. Obesity has become so prevalent that decrying it is seen as being unfair and insensitive. Among many it is a total change of lifestyle and diet that is involved if they are to achieve their goals and for many it is a step too far. Also, for many eating is a pleasure; a pastime to offset so much that is pure drudgery and boredom in their lives. It is hard to give it up and adhere to a regime that gives no satisfaction and becomes yet another cross to bear.

Along with a poor diet has to be added all those other causes which sap the resolve to change ways that are part of life. Cheap but tasty fatty foods, lack of regular exercise, lack of recreation facilities for the young, the Scottish culture of booze and now drugs. Social problems associated with housing, single motherhood, divorce and unemployment. The causes could go on and on with anxiety and depression looming large for many, especially in financially stringent times. Such multiple causes sap morale, inducing laziness and slothfulness while stifling determination. Children brought up in this environment stand a good chance of becoming overweight, especially with TV and the internet replacing physical activity and often poor parental supervision. The thought of developing diabetes and its repercussions for their future lives probably never crosses their mind.

So what is to be done to stop this inexorable progress to a bloated, fat society? For many the deterioration has gone too far and apart from some intrusive surgery there is little hope for a bright tomorrow. For those gross enough and in a way fortunate enough there are some resources set aside in the NHS to offer some hope. The most common is the application of a band around the top of the stomach which makes the patient feel satisfied when the top pocket is full. This can be successful, but there is always the danger of the band slipping and inducing complications. Patients turned down by the NHS have opted to go to the continent for such treatment, but without any subsequent follow up it can be a hazardous procedure, resulting at times in emergency referral back into our health service.

At present there is an increasing waiting list for the operation in the UK, but the question arises, in a dire financial climate, as to whether this is a justifiable use of money. The moral issue of whether people who have brought obesity on themselves deserve to be treated before others with more deserving problems remains to be resolved. Even in my student days we had surgeons who refused to operate on patients with duodenal ulcers unless they undertook to stop smoking, so this type of dilemma is not new. The alternative argument that treated obese patients reduce the need for more expensive medicines and surgery in future is the other side of the coin, making for an unresolved debate.

If the grossly and dangerously overweight are the ultimate group, then the next level must be those who are dramatically heavy, but still able to get about and even work. These along with the many less glaringly obese, who seem unable to lose weight despite all their efforts, also present a formidable challenge. Many people appear to get to a point where everything they try seems to be accompanied by little or no improvement, giving rise to frustration, sinking them into a state of despondency. This group requires encouragement and a continuity of surveillance which seems at present very patchy. Whereas the anti-smoking battle could be fought mainly by propaganda alone, this level of obesity requires a huge input by the individual, community services and the state to provide support, encouragement and continuing surveillance.

Blending into the previous group, we are still left with a

huge proportion of the moderately overweight that will probably get gradually worse, affecting their health in later years and who need action now.

The incentives to eat wisely are all around us and the warnings of the consequences to themselves and even more importantly their children are never far from the headlines. The government has even contemplated paying the obese to slim down, a suggestion which has been met with a barrage of complaints from others who see this as an abuse of tax payer's money. There is little doubt that the carrot is the present approach most favoured by the authorities, but I believe the stick must be also applied now to get results among a certain group of people.

A new initiative suggests that increasing the price of fatty and high calorie foods would make people eat more wisely. The carrot here might be to use this increase in price to allow some subsidising of the more healthy products to lower their prices. This presumes that the public as a whole take responsibility, for both their own and their children's health seriously. Although this may be true for a sizeable proportion, I am sad to say that those probably requiring most assistance will remain either immune or unable to grasp the urgency and will fall by the wayside.

Food manufactures, like the smoking lobby before them, would be up in arms, as recently seen in an interview with the US medical adviser to Coca Cola. Defending the indefensibly high level of sugar in ordinary coke, she in my opinion was telling total untruths, which in this country should have had her up in front of the General Medical Council as unworthy of the medical profession.

Similarly, the chocolate manufacturers would use similar tactics and as a latent choc addict I know how difficult it can be to control the craving. The question of the right of government to interfere in our everyday eating habits raises a moral dilemma, but I feel the consequences for our young and not so young are so grim, that our leadership would be failing in its duty to society not to tackle the problem head on and I would fully back any such initiative.

Having spent my early career in hospitals where obesity was never a factor, as all staff was expected to be smart and trim, to experience our present day set-up is like night after day. The matrons of yesteryear would turn in their graves to view our modern NHS where a consultant told me, sotto voce, he knew when he had blotted his copy book when the administrator sent him another batch of sixteen-stone replacements. I have witnessed, as a patient, one member of staff so fat she had to sit down after making two beds.

To single out one overweight nurse as an example is a bit like admonishing one private soldier in a wholesale raggle-taggle army. It is not the foot soldier who is to blame, but the officer corps and up to the generals who set the criteria. There is a growing sense that leadership is failing, that standards continue to slip, despite all the monotonous trite reassurances and that priorities have changed to a regime with a totally different set of priorities.

The NHS is where the health of the nation starts and where the state should be planning to set an example in tackling this epidemic of the gross. Recognising that many hospitals might have to close if we brought in a health standard of acceptance of say, ten per cent over ideal weight, there is no reason why this should not be the target set for new recruits – doctors, nurses, ancillary staff, etc.. Only by taking a stand is there the stimulus to reach such a reasonable weight. Meanwhile it is ludicrous that we accept without comment the reality of the potentially unhealthy caring for the unhealthy – a damning indictment when with a little vision this could be sensibly tackled.

A howl of protest goes up that this is an intrusion on individual rights, but then we set standards for the Armed Forces and the Police, and after all this is for the individual's future health, so such woolly arguments should be quickly dismissed. Whether our leaders have the will to start setting such targets, especially in times of financial crisis, is unlikely, but there is no excuse for not adopting such an approach in the near future. This initiative could then be applied to other occupations, so stimulating more and more citizens to realise that to get employment, health standards as well as qualifications were essential.

The problem with children is even more urgent, but again

there is a half-hearted approach by the authorities. The provision of improved sporting and outdoor recreational pursuits for the young should become a major priority for our educationalists. Sessions given over to physical exercise should be extended in schools, while recognising that competitive sports, especially for boys, have a great attraction and should be extended and encouraged. The involvement of parents in assisting in these sessions is of the utmost importance. With the health of their children at stake the advice must be strong enough to motivate the most indolent of adults. An increased propaganda campaign targeted at parents, highlighting not only the hazard of diabetes and what that means, but all the other potential health areas which will afflict their children and eventually shorten their lives, should be aimed to bring home to them their own huge responsibilities.

Sadly, there is a feeling that leadership in this obesity epidemic is lacking direction and determination, despite all its potential hazards being fully understood and that only when the tip of the diabetic iceberg emerges more fully will panic set in, but all too late for some.

Finally, the problem of bulimia nervosa could be said to be linked to obesity. Along with the related anorexia nervosa, bulimia is on the increase among young men as well as women. Not fully understood in my day and often very resistant to treatment, it could have unfortunate links to obesity's propaganda.

The symptoms are described as binge eating followed by compensatory behaviours such as vomiting, fasting, using laxatives, enemas, diuretics and over exercising. The mental background appears related to low self esteem, depression, stress, puberty and cultural and social perceptions. The latter could be driven by the vision of the slender models of the fashion industry, so developing an obesity obsession resulting often in gross emaciation and sadly even death. A society hell bent on stamping out disfiguring fatness could be the very trigger to push certain vulnerable youngsters into the bulimia problem, so nothing is without its hazards to someone.

The latest statistic of boys under the age of fifteen in Scotland finds one in ten rated as morbidly obese, so this conundrum is really crying out for a solution, but where is the pioneering determined leadership to come from to tackle it?

SEXUALITY AND RAPE

"THE REPRODUCTION OF MANKIND IS A
GREAT MARVEL AND MYSTERY. HAD GOD
CONSULTED ME IN THE MATTER I SHOULD
HAVE ADVISED HIM TO CONTINUE THE
GENERATION OF THE SPECIES BY FASHIONING
THEM OUT OF CLAY"

MARTIN LUTHER (1483-1546)
Initiator of the Protestant Reformation in Germany

A previous chapter attempted to espouse some charity to those
priests seen by society as having transgressed common

humanity. This chapter looks at sexuality, but in particular at two areas of activity which are associated with much discussion, heat and genuine anxiety. These are subjects, however, that deserve to be viewed as dispassionately as possible, while we try to understand the various motivations behind them.

Human life reduced to its bare bones, as for all other living things, comes down to the survival of the species. This certainly, up to the present time, has depended on sexual activity to produce the next generation. IVF and similar procedures have paved the way to short cut this interaction between male and female for infertility reasons and may eventually herald the dawning of doing without the participating male in the future, but thankfully this has not yet come to pass.

Human beings have been shown through the ages to get up to some bizarre initiatives around the sexual act and it is a fascinating subject to study for those with such an interest. Despite most of us disclaiming any outward interest, our media knows better. Not only did the late *News of the World* have a captive readership, but our daily and week-end heavies know that stories on sex also sell newspapers through all tiers of society.

The burgeoning practice of homosexuality is at present never far from the news, both within our churches and out into the wider community, where proponents do not shy away from promoting their cause. Looked at dispassionately, why should it cause a problem and what are the implications from it in a modern society?

This confusing activity, although having been recorded throughout history, only really came to my notice when studying the war poets from World War I (1914-18). The joy of reading their work was somewhat modified by the sense of unreality, with some such soldiers being war heroes when the popular concept was of effeminate men more at home by the fireside than engaged in a bitter conflict.

A career dealing intimately with the public as a doctor carried me through 36 years without ever knowingly coming upon the practice of homosexual or lesbian behaviour. This seems rather amazing, as it is estimated by the experts that some 10 percent of the population are homosexual, so why did I not become more aware of such a condition when dealing so closely with patients' health? Many outside medicine, however, did perceive it and this was transmitted in the odd nudge or wink at some poor chap who did not quite fit the mould of those around him. A friendly arm around a companion would bring forth ribald remarks from others, so making sure I kept my hands by my side the next time or be branded as you know what forever by some kindly soul.

The last decades have seen such changes in behaviour that could never have been contemplated by dour North-East Scots. Kissing and hugging over such trivialities as scoring a goal at soccer among a bunch of young men who are not exactly schooled in the art of the emotions, is unbelievable. Even among male family members the hearty masculine handshake has given way to an embrace – something it takes time to get used to. I never shirked a close embrace from my female friends, but such a greeting from their male counterparts seems very strange.

Social change has crept up on us in so many different areas. I can still remember the shock and disbelief when one of my upstanding patients ran off with his secretary. The world in my West End practice was aghast, but within a further decade such an event scarcely deserved comment. Similarly with our young, cohabitating outside marriage was taboo from as long as I can remember, but like desertion and divorce became the norm for the young and even the not so young.

The homosexual culture seemed to appear during this savage wind of change, to blow away so many of our preconceived ideas of regular behaviour. It has now gone from a grudging acceptance to almost a cult way of life in this 21st century, which is quite astonishing. It must have been present far more than anyone realised, but it was only thought of as related to the Bohemian set, most obviously after the 1914-18 war. Then it had no relevance to ordinary hard-working poor people and was beyond our imaginations; but when one stops to reflect, it probably has been with us from time immemorial.

A simplistic view of the problem is that we all exist on a sliding scale of sexuality, depending on the ratio of our circulating oestrogen and testosterone hormones. Hopefully, most of us fall just firmly enough into one group or another without being at the extreme ends, which may produce such dangers as rabid rapists. Into these groupings come lesbians and homosexuals, who somehow find themselves on the wrong side of the fence from where nature should have placed them. Some fall so close to the borderline that they themselves find it difficult to know where they fit in. This may explain why some start off with normal marriages before finding their true identity.

Scientifically there is widespread uncertainty among experts as to the true cause and how much of this is genetically based, or may be acquired in the development of the foetus. Researchers tackling the problem from both the biological and psychological aspects have come up with a bewildering number of findings, none of which give a clear-cut answer. An interesting statistic regarding identical twins shows that if one twin is homosexual, the other is also likely to be so affected, suggesting a link to genetic inheritance.

The effect of the early environment on the child's psychological development is also thought to play some part, especially, if as in colour blindness, the degree of homosexuality varies across a wide spectrum of severity from the flamboyant exhibitionist to the vaguely uncertain whose future attitude still hangs in the balance. It goes without saying however that whatever the degree such sexual deviation could be a devastating experience for the individual especially in our past conformist society, but changing times have allowed such people to "come out".

My own particular anxiety however relates to the cultural and environmental influences surrounding homosexuality, which may be playing some part in arresting or aggravating normal maturing in the uncertain young, leaving them stranded in this no man's land of albinism.

Sexual drives, other than those to sustain the species, are abnormal; just as my colour defect would never have brought forth the Impressionists or even traffic lights, so their lifestyle, if predominant, would eliminate the human species eventually. Probably a concept beyond credibility, but none the less demonstrates the futility of accepting this as in any way normal. We have to accept our fate, but not glorify it. Drawing attention to their genetic/acquired problem is divisive in that the community at large thinks of it as a rather freakish condition; glorifying it simply alienates many who do not try to understand.

Many eminent people still do not accept such a condition as a normal abnormality and cannot conceive that it may be genetically no different from left handedness or colour blindness. Witness the soul-searching in the Scottish and Anglican churches over whether such priests are acceptable, even in today's more liberal climate. If many fine brains still find it difficult to come to terms with the condition, then the gay community should quietly enjoy their freedom and live discreetly. They should think carefully about rallies and demonstrations which only highlight differences which at the end of the day are about the loss of a basic human essential, that of procreating as a normal function.

Finally, in this very personal view of homosexuality I find myself troubled by the adoption of children into this unnatural environment. Children have enough trouble growing up in a normal family without the uncertainties presented by gender anomalies. I have no doubt of the loving and caring conditions of such families, but I would require a great deal of evidence before I would ever accept this as being in the long term interests of children.

Much like elderly women opting for treatment to have children in their declining years, this suggests total selfishness, wishing to have a natural lifestyle in abnormal circumstances. The cruel but realistic suggestion that they should buy a puppy instead, may seem unfeeling, but is nevertheless honest advice.

Turning to that other unsettling and unsatisfactory topic related to sexuality is the problem of whether intercourse has been consensual or not. Many women appear to regard this as an open and shut case, while appearing to have little concept of what they are dealing with and no understanding of the forces of sexual turbulence.

Hearing many mature, leading figures in the world of women's rights describe rapists as savages, brings a smile to my lips. All men are savages when it comes to sex; admittedly some are more gentlemanly with it, but with a few drinks or drugs, even the most genteel can be fired by their primitive instincts. To say 'no' is then like holding back the Niagara Falls. The male drive to copulate is no culturally developed piece of civilisation, but has been in our loins since we descended from the trees and long before that. It is probably the most instinctive and important thing we do in life. Eating and drinking may seem essential, but only to keep us alive to achieve our destiny.

Mignon McLaughlin (1913-1983), American journalist and author, summed up the differences for her sex to mull over, very perceptively. Desire in men is a hunger – in women only an appetite. This is a polite quote, whereas that ancient saying, which I can find no one claiming – an erect penis has no conscience – is the brutally frank message. Only once lust has been assuaged does conscience, common sense and often regret return. For some this will herald a clash with the law; for others the undermining of previous relationships or the destabilising of marriage.

The heightening of sexual drive in men builds up inexorably to be only temporarily relieved by ejaculation. This desire is thus satisfied in the young active male for minutes, in the middle-aged for hours, even days, and in the elderly possibly for weeks. This constant craving results in many men having totally indiscriminative liaisons with any available woman, while also being the backdrop for possible sexual abuse.

In contrast the female hormonal cycle – attached to a more considered approach, linked to a subconscious wish to select the most attractive, powerful male available for the sake of her unborn children – makes the scattergun need of the male to copulate haphazardly, quite alien to women's perceptions. Mysteriously, despite this accepted explanation by psychologists, there is no lack of ladies all too prepared to assuage man's selfish, primitive hunger.

This concept is rarely put so baldly in sophisticated circles, so perhaps women are still unaware how much men need self control when stimulated. I cringe when I hear women leaders upholding the right of young ladies to turn up in dance halls, night clubs and pubs scantily dressed. I shall leave the question as to why they would want to flaunt themselves so daringly in such venues, hanging in the air. However, I wonder how many of these ladies would light a cigarette then fill their car with petrol, or wander through an explosives factory with a lighted match to see the way. Crazy, you would say, but that is exactly the risk young women take when parading in this coquettish fashion. Added to our binge drinking culture with possible drugs, it may make for an exciting high life, but the prospect of sexual abuse is never far away for the naïve, nor even the not-so-naïve.

Date rape has been with us from prehistoric times; in the past I have understood it to mean the attempt to have intercourse with a female companion against her will. Some now term it drug-facilitated sexual assault with the emphasis on the word drug, but I feel certain most rape cases in the past were the males simply chancing their luck. My mother had a favourite expression – a man to try, the lady to deny. I doubt if many of my own student generation have not experienced circumstances that could lead to some young women claiming unwelcome attention.

It is a legal minefield with both sides failing to appreciate the other's point of view. In the present day when sex seems taken for granted and practised, I am in no position to judge, except to say that education should stress to young women that if they want to play with fire, they should not expect their male partners to be carrying the fire extinguisher.

Sexual drive among young males varies so significantly that generalised comment on their possible behaviour is worthless; a very small proportion of women have an unusually attractive sexual allure which many men find irresistible. Such attractiveness has been noted as starting occasionally at a very young age in girls, which may account for some cases of child abuse, especially in a family or close community setting.

This whole field of sexuality is surrounded by priggish dishonesty and hypocrisy, with plenty tales of eminent men and women whose own past lives don't justify their damning condemnation of the philandering poor. Prostitution is something we in the leafy suburbs look on as totally foreign.

The term 'the oldest profession in the world' is no joke, as sexual need is always there to be satisfied one way or another. Local authorities may well wish to sweep red light districts from their streets, but without the insight that some in society will always require this service, and planning accordingly, nothing will ever improve.

Serious rape of a stranger falls, in my opinion, into a different and frightening category. Serial rapists come in many forms, but it is probably their temperaments, probably psychotic, linked to unusual sexual drives which combine to make them uncontrollable. Driven by these dark forces they lose all sense of decency and civilised behaviour to assuage their sexual hunger. This may be related to unusually high levels of testosterone and poses the question whether it is their condition that drives them and not evil, as is often professed by the media.

I do not have the expertise to form a judgement, but if rapists having served their jail sentences are counselled and find they cannot help themselves, a further prison sentence may be inappropriate. Certainly re-offending after a prison sentence should trigger the need to consider some form of neutering, as the culprit is a danger not only to others, but to his own peace of mind. Removing the sexual drive could bring back his sanity and make certain that future danger to the public was removed. Only the experts know the full picture, but it does strike me that those whose sexual function is out of control require medical assistance, rather than leaving untreated a condition which may recur with hideous consequences.

While trying to be objective about this problem, there are people involved in abuses that are socially beyond the pale and deserve little or no tolerance. Gang rape, for instance, escalates the problem to a different level; surely a frightening prospect for a civilised society, it defies any solution from the uninformed.

Rape as a weapon of war has now entered our consciousness with the Balkans and Africa bringing the horror of such barbarity to our notice. The long term effects of such depravity are still unclear, with the great danger that they come to be overlooked as affairs of state predominate. Just as we quietly ignore the suffering of the deprived, or the hopelessness of those losing their loved ones in mass killings, so the victims of repeated rape hide themselves away out of sight, and so also out of our thoughts.

Now considering paedophilia, we see the perpetrators as animals, whereas hormonal imbalance along with a personality disorder may well be a significant cause. I am hesitant about the heavy hand of the law in dealing with them, as I have an uneasy feeling we are dealing with basic bodily and mental problems, rather than these people being essentially evil. The fact that so many Roman Catholic priests have been caught up in this scandal points very firmly to their pledge of celibacy affecting their sexual drives, so deviating them into child abuse. If such men of God can be affected against all their basic principles, it is little wonder that in the wider society many unstable minds are caught up in this perversion.

The advent of the internet has also opened the door to mass pornography, including child porn. The number of people caught up in this activity is quite frightening, with an estimated 750,000 child sexual predators across the world. While pornography itself is not illegal in the UK, child porn attracts the heavy hand of the law, with confiscation of the material, registration on the Sexual Offenders List and a possible five-year prison sentence, while distributors are liable to be shut away for up to ten years. A very rough estimate of the profits from only this section of porn is between three and twenty billion dollars a year, so it is a hugely worthwhile venture for the instigators. Sadly, with millions of viewers providing billions more dollars of profit for adult pornography, the problem seems at present beyond the ability of nations to control. It must be a serious worry for parents that our young become seriously addicted.

The problem of internet grooming of the young for sexual liaisons is something which we of the older generation find hard to contemplate. These types of abuses will no doubt become still more serious as the internet and cell phone technology become ever more sophisticated, so the authorities will have their hands full just keeping abreast of the perverts' techniques.

This chapter is driven by the sense that we often make

judgements that are driven by feelings of revenge and misplaced retribution, when we barely understand the problems or our own bodies. Masturbation is not a subject any of us are very comfortable with, but it has seen a sea change in attitudes over a generation. I was presented with *The Mastery of Sex* by my mother when I was about 14, with no further explanation other than to read it carefully for the future. Published in 1931 and written by the Rev. Leslie D. Weatherhead, I see it now described by a critic as a book with a lovely sense of naivety. We have come a long way since then, but I always remember masturbation described as an abuse of the body and an unchristian act, which terrified me at the time.

Eighty years later the medical profession views it totally differently, with talk of it reducing prostate cancer and keeping the sperms fresh and active for when proper intercourse with a family in mind occurs. Its ability, in both sexes, in reducing sexual tension and relieving depression is well recognised, while a lowering of blood pressure has also been recorded. Its effectiveness, especially in young men, in releasing emotions that could lead to more cases of especially date rape, has been postulated. Thankfully, we are shut away in our own private lives with this embarrassing subject, but evidence shows over 90 percent of men and up to 70 percent of women have used this method at some time in their lives, but never a word of it is whispered in polite society.

This whole field of sexual behaviour requires careful

thought and understanding. The heavy hand of the law descending on those downloading child pornography without any sign of their doing anything criminal is rather puzzling. Titillating magazines have been available for years, with individuals having their own particular fetishes. Despite its unpleasantness and degrading associations, it will be interesting in future to understand why dealing with such as child pornography without any actual child involvement is illegal, while outlandish and debasing adult pornography remains acceptable.

The sad scenes of irate parents besieging some innocent stranger in his house, because someone rumoured he was a paedophile, is perhaps understandable, but it is a poor reflection on our society when we are still no better than an ignorant lynch mob. I feel the media has a grave responsibility in distorting public opinion in this field. Organised crimes, such as burglary, are crimes of choice, whereas most sexual crimes may be due to malfunction of the human body and mind. Are we guilty of using the wrong standards to judge such people? Future generations may well look back at our shutting such people up in prison in the same way as we now perceive our forebears burning so-called witches at the stake.

The problems of sexual activity, including homosexuality, but especially rape and paedophilia, are highly emotive with a wide spectrum of opinion and prejudice. I feel strongly it is the duty of the media to stop running these cases as high drama, titillating the public, but to bring calmness and perspective to bear so that the whole field of sexuality can come to be more readily understood.

Finally there are some wonderful sayings regarding sex, mostly with tongue in the cheek humour. Bette Davis (1908–1989) American actress of film, television and theatre quotes, "Sex is God's joke on human beings", while Rita Rudner, American comedienne, actress and writer born 1953 follows up with, "Men reach their sexual peak at 18; women reach theirs at 35. Do you get the feeling that God is playing a practical joke?".

No doubt somewhere up there Martin Luther is still chastising God for getting it all wrong – clay would certainly have simplified life and done away altogether with this chapter, but then deprived so many of those highlights of their lives.

Driving Me Mad

**ROAD SENSE IS THE OFFSPRING OF
COURTESY AND THE PARENT OF SAFETY**

AUSTRALIAN TRAFFIC RULE

It all started with a visit to Hamleys. For those who do not recognise the name, make sure the next time you are in London to proceed to Regent Street and you will find a shop that is an absolute wonderland of toys. If you are accompanied by your children, or perhaps grandchildren, you should be prepared to have a difficult time extricating yourself without spending a small fortune.

As I was an only precious child, my father had popped into Hamleys on his way home from one of the laird's big trips abroad to bring me a lovely pedal-propelled Rolls-Royce. Looking back at the photographs of that era, the year would have been 1931-2 when I was about three and just able to reach the pedals to get it moving. It was a truly exotic toy for a working-class family and my chums would gather round daily for a 'shottie' or call me a spoiled brat or worse when I refused.

Hamleys' catalogue was sent every year to Lord Glentanar's family and when it was due to be thrown out my father salvaged it for me, so that by the time war broke out in 1939 I had accumulated eight well-thumbed copies. I can still recall dull, rainy days when stuck in the house I would sit on the floor in front of my little toy cupboard and spend hours poring over the pages. The Rolls-Royce was the high water mark as far as Hamleys was concerned, though; I could spend hours wishing, but my father seemed to think that enough was enough even if I was precious.

That little car gave years of pleasure and the family album still has me pedalling furiously up to the age of six. Seven saw me graduate to a Hercules bicycle and here again my chums would gather round as even their fathers often had not yet graduated to owning such a modest mode of transport.

1937 was, however, the really magical year when my father made it out of the cloth-capped working class and was elevated to a somebody in the district. A shiny black, brand new Austin 10 arrived at our door on a June day that year and my father achieved a life-long ambition. Over the years it would make the trip to France, while in the winter it slithered around our ice-bound roads, frequently meeting an awkward telegraph pole or other impediment, once managing to somersault down a railway embankment. Surviving without a scratch, my father would dutifully have all the dents painstakingly repaired so that the machine was always in pristine condition.

The war years came in 1939 and living five miles from the nearest village, petrol coupons were available. The headlights shrouded in black flanged metal filters made driving a really trying experience at night, especially as my father was never more than a very mediocre driver. As the war drew to its close, my desire to get behind the wheel saw my father relenting and allowing me to drive around the estate's private roads. By 17 I had my licence – no need at that time to take a test – and the world was opening up for me. My father had huge patience, never lost his temper and even when I failed to drain off the water from the radiator one winter's night and ice caused the cylinder head to split, he took it all in his stride and scarcely admonished me. I think he realised there was no one more sick with disgust than myself and a row in these circumstances was unnecessary.

Returning from National Service in 1957 and being temporarily without a car, the old Austin would chug around Aberdeen as I did a stint as a locum GP before returning to hospital practice. A rudimentary machine by the 1950s, but my father ignored all my pleadings to replace it with a beautiful

Sunbeam Talbot 90 and so it continued until that fateful day in 1968. My father, now 87 years old, had become an even more erratic driver and I was terrified every time he came to visit us twenty miles away. I was surprised that his doctor continued to allow him to drive, while my mother would get greatly annoyed with me if I suggested he was becoming a hazard to them both. The car was a lifeline for her to get away for one day every week to do her shopping and she just closed her eyes to the dangers.

That Sunday evening, the parents having left us to depart for home, I was oblivious to everything watching England play Germany in the football World Cup. England one goal up and all was going superbly when the telephone rang to say that both parents were in hospital with multiple injuries. My father had misjudged the speed of the oncoming traffic and turned into the path of a Mini, causing fractured limbs and ribs to both him and my mother, but thankfully causing no injuries to those in the Mini. Seeing them comfortably settled in hospital, I returned home to receive the final blow of finding that the Germans had won yet again.

Although my father recovered to live another 10 years, his driving days were over and the Austin was scrap metal. Now 82 years old myself, I am acutely aware of the hazards of driving as the years march on and I am ever watchful for signs of deterioration in my own standards.

Over my career I have had an inferiority complex, never

having taken a driving test; I have always felt I was in no position to criticise others when my abilities had never been tested. I have driven a wonderful range of machines through the years and love the exhilaration of a smooth, fast machine, having cut my milk teeth on motor cycles. This thrill has gone on with me up to the present time. Watching others who have passed their tests driving like beginners, I decided to join the Advanced Drivers' Association some years ago and revelled in passing the rigorous test with flying colours. Now in the perfect position to point out the foibles of other drivers, I think the advanced test should be the standard before any driver is accepted as fully qualified.

I am intrigued with the Australian system which seems so much more demanding than our own. In Victoria the young people get their provisional L-plates at 16 years of age and must pass a car learner permit test. They then go on to practice until at age eighteen they sit their proper driving test. Within these two years they must complete a log book recording 120 hours or more of driving, of which 10 hours must be at night. The log book is completed by the qualified driver who is supervising the learner.

Once they have passed their test they are allowed to drive, but must exhibit a red P-plate for a minimum of one year. This then changes to a green P-plate for three years, when it can be removed. A poor driving record extends the P1 and P2 stages by six months or more. While on red P-plates they are not allowed to carry passengers under 16 years of age, unless immediate family members, and may carry only one passenger aged between 16 and 22, as many accidents occur with groups of youths in one car. There is also zero alcohol tolerance in these stages. The effect of all this, other than making the young realise they are still beginners, is to alert other drivers that these P-plate holders are relatively inexperienced. Police take a far stricter approach to the P-plate over minor transgressions in order to reinforce the lesson of attaining skill.

It is worth pausing for a moment to marvel at the ability of the average human being to control tons of lethal metal. When you consider the volume of traffic and think of all the different personalities behind the wheel, it becomes a frightening thought. As a doctor I can scarcely believe that some people are capable or even, dare I say it, intelligent or responsible enough to be allowed to be in control of such a deadly object. Police go to extraordinary lengths to check whether a person is mentally capable of owning a gun licence, but in many ways the car driver is far more dangerous and there are millions more of them.

Some drivers are totally competent, but a huge proportion fall into the category of borderline basic drivers. In addition, many may be driving with disabilities, some acute, others chronic, which do not require the supervision of the medical profession. Total concentration may be ours one day, but not the next. There are the drivers angry after an altercation with their spouse or employer, those who are late for an appointment, those distracted with worry or anxiety, chatting to their passenger or fiddling with the radio control, or the farmer more interested in whether his neighbour has started cutting his crop. So much intrudes on our minds, such as family stresses as we rush to pick up the children from school, but with only half our attention on the world around us. These diversions on our attention are never-ending and all potentially deadly.

A number of drivers offset some of the hazards by insulating themselves in 4x4s, and bullying those in lesser machines to back off from confrontation. Others bully lesser mortals into giving way both by speed and intrusive manoeuvring. In many ways these motorists are very accomplished, but it is when the less endowed attempt the same that dangers arise.

The more mundane mistakes that occur daily are so repetitive that the authorities show poor perception in allowing them to persist. The basic tenet of advanced motoring is that drivers should be thinking of every other motorist as incompetent, being capable of all forms of basic mistakes at any time. This then develops the defensive strategy of the advanced motorist to expect and watch for anything that remotely looks like a hazard. Reading not only the road ahead, but the road behind is vital in this training. Assessing the weather and road conditions also plays its part. Obeying the rules of the road, such as speed restrictions or other signals, can irritate even the best of drivers, but once you accept that you are an expert then you feel only regret when you transgress occasionally. The best of us can make occasional mistakes as none of us are infallible, but I personally suffer agonies for days after if I sense that I have misjudged a situation and resolve never to let that one happen again.

On the whole I feel reasonably satisfied with the behaviour of other road users towards me. They allow me access from a side road quite quickly, and allow me to overtake when they are obviously travelling more slowly than me. Sensitive drivers also recognise certain marques of car and more readily make way for some than others. Harassed by a Jaguar on my tail is much more threatening than some clapped-out old Nissan.

The most trying daily hazard is the tailgater who only needs me to touch my brakes hard to have him/her coming through my boot. I look in my mirror and try to gauge who is behind the wheel. Is it some old chap who is no longer quite aware of what he is doing, or is it some young lady, blissfully unaware that she is liable to have to meet her costs and mine from a nasty coming together? It may be some aggressive young man sending me a distinct message that I am in his way and he will continue to terrorise me until I let him past. Unhappily most bumper drivers are just run-of-the-mill motorists who are trying to get from A to B in the shortest length of time and have an unfailing faith that I am not suddenly going to stamp on my brakes.

I am astonished that so many drivers are unaware of the three-second safety rule which should be a must for everyone. From the first recognition of trouble ahead to the driver's reaction to that trouble, three seconds pass. No matter the type of road or the speed you are travelling, this is the minimal reaction time. Adverse weather conditions or higher driving speeds need more time, so counting three seconds from the time the car in front passes that telegraph pole to you reaching the pole count three seconds and see if you would have hit him.

I use this test driving at 30 mph and tend to stay even further back now, as I am sure my reaction time is gradually slowing up and the fright of a sudden braking ahead is just not something I relish. I hesitate to stick some caustic comment on my car about other people's bad driving in case they stop and assault me, but one I particularly like is RU2Close? If it had the Advanced Driver's logo attached to it, suggesting joining that organisation, I might just use it.

This then brings us to another problem. Some of us drive not only as a necessity, but also as a hobby. I take a pride in driving to a standard that an expert would pass as reasonably sound. A mass of drivers, however, are not in that category and drive from a requirement to reach their work, the shops, for business or pleasure. Some drive to be seen in their open Mercs and BMWs, usually attractive young women with the latest fashion sunglasses across their foreheads. Many young men and some young women drive with too much oomph just to show off and with maturity will lose the thrill of speed. These are the drivers who most need to keep up their standards to avoid accidents, as they fail to perceive that passing the test was merely an entry point to a skill which would take years to cultivate.

Among other basic faults seen daily is poor positioning on the road. Is it my imagination or are those cars sitting well to the left of the midline, but indicating to turn right mostly driven by ladies? Shame on me, but then is the driver at the traffic lights crossing just on the red nearly always a man? I also continue to be amazed in these days of slow-moving, congested traffic that some drivers seem surprised to find that lights do change to green, so by the time they have wakened up only three cars get across before the lights turn back to red.

Most of the mistakes on the road appear to be due to lack of attention or vision. Failure to use indicators is annoying, while headlights seem by some only to be used in the dead of night. So many drivers fail to turn on their lights in bad visibility or in the gloaming, which shows a woeful lack of insight. Asking one lady why she was driving without lights she admitted to not being sure about how to turn them on, but in any case she could see quite clearly – a real candidate for a refresher course.

There is a vigorous argument over whether we should use our headlights or sidelights in built up areas at night. Some argue that the glare of headlights blinds oncoming drivers, especially the aged and in wet conditions, whereas others find seeing a car with only sidelights, while all others are driving on headlights, is a real hazard. I must say that headlights do dazzle, especially the newer variety, and some need to be refocused as even when dipped they are too high. Motorcycles with their headlights permanently on are a huge boon to motorists, especially as that fraternity can appear from nowhere at high speed, so I tend to agree with the argument for headlight use by motorists more often than not.

The danger of being unaware of faults in one's car is especially relevant to headlights, indicators and braking lights. The need for all manufactures to alert drivers to failed lights as well as more major faults is essential, as an approaching car with its offside lights out of action is a huge hazard.

I have a real bee in my bonnet over parking. I get furious with the thoughtlessness of the motorist who parks half a length from the end of a marked nose-to-tail area on city streets, so blocking off two spaces. Haphazard positioning all along the marked off section is so common that obviously the owners are oblivious to the needs of others. You would think that seeing their favourite parking spot taken up the next week by some idiotic intruder using up two spaces, the penny would eventually drop – but no such luck.

The seat belt initiative has been a huge success, but there is a huge temptation to answer a ringing mobile in the car, despite the law against a hand-held instrument. Drivers turning down side roads one-handed with a phone in the other can still be observed, so more work has to be done in this field.

I shall not say much on the law of 70mph on a motorway and 60mph otherwise, except for built up area speeds. With petrol prices through the roof I now drive circumspectly and certainly keep to 70mph on a motorway. At this speed I usually never pass another car, but everything passes me. What sort of legislation is this that nobody appears to adhere to?

A résumé of idiosyncratic motorists would be incomplete without a sideways glance at the danglers, those light-hearted souls who embellish their windscreens front and back with distracting dangling objects sending out disturbing signals regarding their competence. However, I do get a sense of friendly derision at my stuffy attitudes with Churchill's bulldog, nodding and grinning at me from that car ahead - Oh YES!

I am sure that good manners breeds good manners in others. The motorist who stops to allow me to draw out from the pavement, or to let me turn right in front of him/her, stimulates me to do the same for someone else half-a-mile further on. This consideration then rubs off on yet another motorist who adopts the same approach further down the road or the next day. The courteous wave of thanks is also a great advert for good driving. Even if only ten per cent learn a lesson each time, then gradually it becomes the norm and we can come to feel real warmth for our fellow drivers.

In the North-East of Scotland, we suffer from the result of

so much car ownership; the mind-deadening traffic jam. Sitting nose to tail in rush hours seems the ultimate in man's stupidity. The maddening thing is that we all sit there like zombies and accept it. If there ever was evidence of society being a mass of followers instead of leaders, this is it. Our planners are reactors, not perceivers, or this situation would have been foreseen and solved before such deadlock was reached. However, as with so much in our nation, our civic leaders and their henchmen find such problems too much for their abilities, but are buffered in the knowledge that the long-suffering public will just put up with yet another layer of inconvenience.

I firmly believe our driving test should consider the Australian P-licence; better still, two years after passing the basic test a compulsory advanced driving test should be taken before full registration is allowed. The standard of driving is still too elementary and only when motorists begin to think more positively and defensively will improvements occur. However, as with so much in our nation, the obvious seems all too difficult or costly for our masters, so horrific road casualties are unlikely to fall any time soon.

Finally, it is well worth remembering that although many of us fall within the regulations in our ability to drive a car, that does not mean we are all of the same effectiveness. This is particularly true of the ageing motorist where both physical and mental faculties are no longer pristine. Eyesight may be acceptable to drive, but is reduced in range and judgement of distance, while reaction times have slowed and a level of uncertainty creeps in with added years. All this is not only relevant to the elderly, but to all motorists. Never take anything for granted and assess every other road user as a potential accident waiting to happen.

Finally, before becoming too swell headed over our advanced driving techniques stop for a moment and view how they do it in India. Having experienced this at first hand the initial shock of total chaos has us holding our heads in despair. As time goes on, however, a pattern emerges which demands that each road user concentrates on avoiding any other obstacle on the road, be it animate or inanimate. Speed of thought and fine judgement are of the essence. Amazingly accidents appear few in daytime despite roads clogged with lorries, cars, scooters, rickshaws, cyclists and pedestrians as well as sacred cows, pigs, goats, sheep and stray dogs around every corner. To our Western eyes huge risks are taken at speed, but there seems a general consensus that as long as every one plays the game of avoidance and gives way as necessary you are even allowed to drive down a two-way highway without anyone getting upset. It certainly can take your breath away, but it does show there is always more than one way to skin a cat.

THE CURSE OF STATUS

"EVERYONE SHOULD BE RESPECTED AS AN INDIVIDUAL BUT NO ONE IDOLISED"

ALBERT EINSTEIN

If you boast a personalised number plate or a prestigious postal code you will enjoy this chapter. Or is it that honorary degree or birthday honours which swells you with pride? Perhaps your golf handicap is something to crow about, but if not then that photo of you standing beside Tiger Woods is your kudos for boasting points at the golf club bar.

Status is defined as standing, position, rank and importance in a society or in a group. It is something as human beings we become aware of from childhood and it stays with us until our last breath.

It all harks back to man's development and how evolution has allowed us to prosper through the ages. Our tiers of leadership and seniority give us, as a nation, a direction and place in the world, while in our homes it is the ingredient hopefully to bring stability and success.

Status is something we all probably yearn for, but often subconsciously. Speak to many people and they will deny they have any desire for status, but when asked specific questions as how they see themselves, it turns out that it is all important. Remember those days in the school playground or football pitch, how we prayed to be one of the first to be picked for all those bounce games and how our self respect could swell when we came to be the first or second selected.

Join any convivial group and someone will be the most talkative, the most argumentative, the story teller or just the one being really pleasant. Yet each one in their own way is putting down a marker, usually quite without realising it, and saying I am distinctive and have my place in this pecking order. Even the silent little lady in the background may quietly say something which suddenly makes others realise that she is not to be ignored and may indeed be quite a threat by observing and not talking.

Yet, mostly when we talk of status we are thinking of those

powerful people in the world who shape great events, as we ourselves are but the faceless, powerless majority. Through the ages men and the occasional woman have been driven by ambition to achieve certain goals and in so doing have acquired great standing and power among their fellow citizens. History has been kind to some in seeing their achievements as beneficial to mankind, whereas others have been vilified as ogres. Increasingly historians are teasing out famous lives from the past with new evidence which paints a totally different picture of our past heroes.

Wealth and status are often seen as synonymous and this is particularly true where inequality of wealth is greatest, as in the two most affluent Western countries – the USA and the UK. Income differences in Japan and some Scandinavian countries are such that the richest 20 percent are less than four times as rich as the poorest, while in Singapore, USA & the UK the richest 20 percent are about nine times richer than the poorest.

In the UK much has changed through the last decades, but often only superficially. The layers of class distinction seem less demarcated, so that far more now see themselves as middle class. The top and bottom of society do not change, however, with too many of us still paying lip service to our betters or the famous. Titles and honours are doled out routinely, with the great majority of the meaningful ones going to the privileged. We pride ourselves as being one of the foremost democracies in the world, but our leaders continue to make certain that they still get the largest slice of the cake. You scratch my back and I'll scratch yours is still prevalent in far too many walks of life.

So how does status make a difference to us in our everyday lives? Observe our Prime Minister David Cameron conducting the affairs of state. With his moneyed background and education at Eton and Oxford University, he exudes the confidence of a man born to lead. Money has given him status, Eton has reinforced it and just to make doubly sure, he attends one of the foremost educational establishments in the world. Is he a heavyweight, or just another high born product of a system which makes it impossible to tell his true worth? To be born into the aristocracy ensures status whether you are bright or stupid, rich or scraping the barrel. No-one can take away your pedigree.

For those of less distinguished backgrounds there are layer upon layer of differences within the so-called class structure of the nation. My father's employment graded him as working-class, but in his own eyes he was right at the top of that grade. He conducted himself as a gentleman and when on holiday we stayed in the best hotels and ate in the most salubrious of restaurants. He never deigned to wear a cloth cap as this really would put him down among the labourers and he would smoke Churchman's No 1 cigarettes and Havana cigars and none of your cheap rubbish. He was no snob, but he valued his status as a true professional in his trade and was proud to have the respect of his peers.

Although he was proud of his achievements from being a poor uneducated farm boy, he always said he wanted his son to be a £1,000 a year man. Back in the 1930s this level of income was the golden target associated with the earnings of a gentleman, and a university education was the surest route to such a target. The professions have always exuded status, so my entry into medicine achieved my father's ambitions for his son.

There is little doubt that the professions open the door to status, but before that my years at Aberdeen Grammar School also ensured status. Wherever I go I find the fact that I have attended that school makes me a member of a select club, which has had many advantages for me throughout my career. Here we come up against the thorny problem of privilege; with status so important, it is understandable that those inside the big tent are keen to keep the status quo.

For many years I found my humble beginnings almost an embarrassment, but gradually with maturity and insight I have become proud of my background, and especially of my parents who made all things possible. As for myself as regards status, I now take it for granted. Having escaped from medical practice without blotting my copy book and now having become an author, no matter how insignificant, I can sit back contentedly and watch others trying to make their mark.

Always having tried to be of an independent mind, I view many of our aspirations at climbing the greasy pole with interest.

The personalised or distinctive number plate is a prime example. I have owned a distinctive plate for years, the result of a trade deal, and I leave it to the reader to consider its significance. I have sympathy for those owning really opulent cars giving such machines some individuality instead of letters and numbers which only tell the onlooker how old they are. The status of such drivers requires no comment from me, as they are declaring how they rate themselves to the world. But why do we lesser mortals with run-of-the-mill vehicles spend good money on such a piece of blatant showmanship?

A piece of fun while overcoming the embarrassment of never being able to remember the original number in awkward situations is a common reason, which stops my analysis in its tracks. It gives the car a more distinctive look and gives me the satisfaction of being different from the common herd. Yet there are numbers which have cost a fortune which do anything but enhance the car. Manufacturers have spent years streamlining and perfecting shape and the owner goes and hangs on a number which is as out of place as a Rolls-Royce Flying Lady on an ancient Austin 7.

So some of us are showing our lack of refined taste, while the quality of the number tells whether the owner is really well off or just able to pay a hundred or two to join this potty status club. Very fancy numbers on BMW and Mercedes 4x4s suggest *nouveau riche*, especially if driven by attractive ladies on the private school run, which is maybe a little unjust.

The psychologist could make a fairly accurate outline of the person's personality in spending time and money to make a statement of so little importance. Is it that the neighbours have one and we must not feel left behind? There are some very funny and clever plates out there which justify their existence, though. As a doctor, one of my favourite ones was held by a colleague in general practice – SAY 99.

Then there are the exhibitionists amongst us. We come in all shapes and forms from the over the top types such as Richard Branson and Lord Alan Sugar to the cantankerous little lady in the corner shop who rules the roost, while we strive to get a smile of approval from her once in a while. Again, many fail to recognise their behaviour as being the need to be recognised as individuals of merit; some will do anything, however absurd, to be kept in the public eye. Many apparently charitable initiatives have behind them the self same desire, although never to be faced up to as such.

Perhaps it is best not to examine too closely our basic motivations to do certain things. I write books and write copious letters to the press in the name of interest and involvement, but how much is really about self promotion? Humans are capable of so many spontaneous acts of decency that it is perhaps best to let these particular sleeping dogs lie and ignore all such unwelcome introspection.

Those of us who own prestigious postcodes or who belong to an exclusive golf club have also much to ponder about. The tale is told that our most select ladies golf club has members clustering around the new entrant with two questions. What does your husband do and where do you live? This is told by critics to illustrate the snobbery of the membership, but although this may be the apparent reason, it is in fact more about where this new member will fit into the hierarchy. Not that the members asking the question realise this, but how they deal with this incomer in future will have been influenced by these two questions. If the third question is about her handicap and the answer is two, that will certainly leave most members trailing in her wake.

My other preoccupation in this field is with titles, the birthday and New Year's honours lists and honorary degrees. Titles, I feel, are a remnant of the Middle Ages and are totally irrelevant in this 21st century. They belong to an age when the monarchy required its layers of courtiers to maintain its authority and preserve the throne, which scarcely has a place in a democratic society. Titles are huge elevators of status, inducing in the average citizen peasant-like respect, whether the recipient deserves it or not. A true patriot of our country, I feel that we, the common people, have let ourselves down by allowing those in power, with so much self interest, to perpetuate this system.

I am a tepid royalist, accepting the benefits of a settled, relatively powerless monarchy, instead of lesser mortals wheeling and dealing to assume power, often for their own ends. I do also recognise the tremendous status the UK achieves throughout the world, its unrivalled pomp and ceremony being our showpiece for others to envy. The benefits, therefore, justify the continuation of the monarchy, but there is a downside which those of us who believe in equality feel uneasy about.

Titled honours I see as being one of the powerful tools of our elite to keep such a monarchic system in place. Cleverly, the establishment has conned the public by handing out knighthoods and peerages to lesser mortals, encouraging the clamour of the plebs to honour celebrity. By elevating an annual quota of commoners above their station, the masses are brainwashed from seeing anything incongruous in the system. As a leading democratic country, we proudly pay lip service to the concept of equality for backward nations while maintaining our own antiquated class structure.

While disagreeing with the concept, it is interesting that a title does not always enhance the status of the recipient. Some distinguished men and women of substance clearly justify recognition, but with a House of Lords requiring a quota of members to give it credibility, relative nonentities can fill the benches making a mockery of the system. So the whole paraphernalia is a farce riddled with anomalies, including the failure to strip recipients of their titles when they fall foul of the law or disgrace themselves and their positions.

For me, some sporting figures have been almost demeaned,

such as a peerage for a runner and knighthoods for a cyclist and a golfer. Genuine sporting heroes are excessively elevated, while others of equal merit are overlooked. Such haphazard titles are, in my view, about bolstering the continuation of an archaic class-based state, with the individuals concerned being simply convenient, compliant tools.

Within the system, however, some do seem to get it right and a past Prime Minister John Major is an excellent example. Offered a peerage he turned it down, but accepted a knighthood instead. In keeping with his persona this seemed sensible, whereas I have no such feelings of appropriateness about the Lords Owen and Lamont. Also the accolade 'Dame' seems much less intrusive, having a cosy motherly feel about it which does soothe a little of my irritation.

The saddest outcome in the use of honours is when those you look up to succumb to the baubles handed down from on high. Aneurin Bevan, son of a Welsh coalmining family and architect of the NHS, would have felt he had betrayed his roots if he had accepted such a symbol from the exclusive upper classes. A working class hero and a man of giant proportions and independent outlook is Alex Ferguson of Aberdeen FC and Manchester United fame. For him to accept the accolade of a knighthood was the moment my pride in my own background was shaken to the core, but I had to accept that in this day and age he probably never paused to consider it a betrayal.

The Queen's twice yearly honours troubles me rather less.

In fact it is the status of the Queen which would be under pressure if we were to abolish such accolades. Like titles, these honours have been spread down the social order to give credibility, but I feel this in itself is flawed. Different layers of honours bring a pecking order of status once again and signals value to the honour which appear quite arbitrary. A far fairer way is to give a single level of honour, leaving it to other societies to recognise service in their specific fields. Too many snouts in the trough will not bring about a quick rethink and an unthinking, servile public does not help.

Honorary degrees also seem to have got out of hand. Holding one such award, I am very proud of it and it probably enhances my status in some quarters, but I do not need any more to boost my ego. Yet universities vie with one another to pour out honorary degrees to people who are already loaded with them. Also jumping on the celebrity bandwagon, academic institutes of great standing confer degrees on the oddest people, suggesting uncertainty at the calibre of their academic committees. Whether they have entered the field with an eye on financial enhancement or have forgotten their original remit, it is depressing to see such institutions joining in this type of behaviour.

One group who have no problem with their status are those with an eye for the beautiful ladies and here is where they really score. No stranger to power and status is Henry Kissinger, who adds his own slant to the quote, "Power is the ultimate aphrodisiac". Going on to explain how the powerful and famous attract females like bees to a honeypot, he no doubt has a certain Miss Monica Lewinsky in mind.

Pictures of the wonderful wives and girlfriends of the Ryder Cup team and those of the World Cup English soccer team show what fame and fortune can do for your chances. For those of us of the older variety it should be remembered that Aristotle Onassis, the not very attractive Greek shipping magnate, married the lovely Jacqueline Kennedy, then only 39 years old, in 1968 when he was 62, so with status and money anything is possible.

Status by association is interesting: whether it is chronic name-dropping in conversation or being seen in the company of our betters, this is one of the commonest forms of trying to improve social standing. Such an elementary ploy is rapidly seen as a charade, so having the opposite effect, resulting in such people being rated as mere adulators. Care has to be taken, however, as many of us almost subconsciously boast of the achievements of our own family members, when justifiable pride can easily be taken for bragging.

Odd outcomes of association do occur, as seen in the present White House. As President Obama's popularity dived, that of his wife Michelle went higher and higher. Not that she was a trophy wife, already being a lawyer; her initial status was as the President's wife, but latterly it was about her own popularity. Eva Peron, an illegitimate child from a poor family, achieved status through marriage to the president of Argentina. But for her premature death she could have become vice president, perhaps even president, such was her popularity with the poor.

So is status a curse or an asset? Those who are blessed to mightily achieve I am sure view it with huge pride. For the more modest individuals, many of us can thank our education for giving us a measure of respect. Many from sheer hard work and dedication or sense of community, in giving their time for the sake of others, have also achieved recognisable status. Status and respect are not static, however, and can be easily lost.

The biggest curse of all has so far been omitted. Human beings are not the most logical, so when things are going badly their morale and self esteem sink into their boots. When the opposite pertains, they get a sense of elation, often accompanied by self grandeur. To watch mediocre retired politicians strutting the stage like ancient peacocks encompasses all that is worst about status. Swollen-headedness is all too evident among those who have achieved fame and fortune, the nouveau riche often exhibiting it with unseemly brashness. The blue bloods are born to status and have no need to trumpet it, but we lesser mortals are not so blessed. From personal experience, it needs little encouragement and flattery to turn a relatively modest individual into a pompous showman. Few from academia, the professions or business escape this disappointing effect. Even our Armed Services are not immune, with routine knighthoods for the upper crust testing their calibre in how they cope with such pomp and glory.

This chapter is simply the opening of a door on a huge and intricate subject. Many lives are driven by this need to be valued, which could be seen as a curse. For those who are aware of the pitfalls, it is a great asset.

Until we abolish a house for lords we shall remain an anachronistic master/serf nation. I do firmly believe in meritocracy, defined as an elite group of people whose progress is based on ability and talent rather than on class privilege or wealth. I sometimes feel as if I am standing on the ramparts of the Bastille rallying the French Republic instead of vainly trying to get my own fellow countrymen to recognise their unthinking servility and waken up to the modern world.

Knowing readers will puzzle why this author with a status-enhancing title like 'Dr' in front of his name should become incandescent about titles for others. Is it right to have medical men and academics happy to accept such accolades, but deny others similar recognition. Why do doctors look askance at dentists who now attach a similar prefix to their names? Yes, these are academic titles achieved after years of study, but is the status acquired from them justified? Perhaps I have to accept that I may subliminally be trying to protect my own treasured status – all very confusing.

Day in, day out, we are all subconsciously involved in this status merry-go-round. For the insightful it is of constant interest, whether watching the great and the good playing the game, or sensing that quiet lady over in the corner with the eagle eye who I bet could tell us all a home truth or two.

PROSPERITY, POLITICS AND PUBLIC OPINION

**"DEMOCRACY IS A DEVICE THAT ENSURES
WE SHALL BE GOVERNED NO BETTER THAN
WE DESERVE"**

GEORGE BERNARD SHAW
(1856-1950)
Irish Playwright and Philosopher, also
Co-founder of the London School of Economics

The wonder of childhood is the pure innocence of it all, while the sadness of old age is the knowledge that innocence is only for the angels.

In my childhood, living on a country estate sheltered from all the vagaries of life in the wider world, we never thought of ourselves as poor, but certainly not as rich. Yet we were in fact tremendously rich, but in a context that none of us would have recognised at the time. We all had enough to eat and drink, we lived in a community that was stable and friendly, while the adults could indulge in a smoke, a little alcohol at times and a social life that fulfilled most needs. As children we had all the fresh air and open space to fulfil our days, while school, although disciplined, was never really seen as a hardship. Holidays, for the average worker, was a day out to the mighty city of Aberdeen, with a visit to the beach with the kids and an ice cream to make their day, or a visit to Woolworths to buy something for sixpence.

We were rich in contentment and ease of living, being totally unaware of how life could be for those millions outwith our domain. Talking to our young nowadays and asking them for their vision of the future, prosperity and possessions seem their priorities in life. No sense that health and happiness have yet entered their orbit, but then perhaps we should leave them to dream for a little longer before the reality of life dawns on them.

Prosperity is something we all hope for, but in the present climate of recession and depression the future for our young is not yet obvious. This brings us to the way we are governed and the abilities of our leaders to steer us through hazardous times.

Always interested in politics, I sense that for years we have been teetering along with our economy struggling to replace our dependency on the heavy industries of the past. Over reliance on the financial sector, with its weakness in making profits out of questionable initiatives, has been badly exposed. Added to this, the Pied Piper-like acceptance that bonuses are the way to stimulate staff to do their job is a sad reflection on human nature. An honest day's work for an honest day's pay is a reflection of Victorian times which has been totally lost in our present day spiv-like culture.

Tony Blair when he became prime minister in 1997 appointed Frank Field to think the unthinkable, to provide the basis for changing the direction of planning in the UK, hopefully making it a better nation for all. Within months of his appointment, however, Mr Field found he was redundant to Labour's image of a fresh start. As with so many empty promises from previous politicians, little changed and some would say some areas even deteriorated.

Margaret Thatcher in a speech in 1987 stated that "There is no such thing as society". This much quoted phrase is generally misunderstood. Thatcher was propounding that the individual should be responsible for himself/herself and not always looking to be helped out by the state providing amenities such as housing. Individuals should have a duty to strive to achieve, while looking out for their neighbours. A society that acts as cotton wool for its members will soon find no one striving to achieve anything, was her stark message. She summed it up beautifully by saying, "there is no such thing as entitlement, unless someone has first met an obligation".

Since then, this has often been demonstrated by the many teenage girls getting themselves pregnant, only with the intention of obtaining council housing, which if true is a tragic state for a civilised nation. Babies being used simply as tools to manipulate regulations is despicable, but then many young women may counter by demonstrating their sheer hopelessness in a world already peopled by the grossly underprivileged.

For politicians the tragedy is that they start out as starry eyed idealists, but the monstrous difficulties they face in government rapidly erode their pioneering spirit. In addition, human beings appear to have great difficulty keeping their feet on the ground once in power which, it seems, can all go too quickly to their heads.

This is no new phenomenon as through the ages historians and parliamentarians have voiced their misgivings. William Pitt the Elder in 1770 in the House of Commons stated "unlimited power is apt to corrupt the minds of those who possess it". Edmund Burke, a famous statesman and philosopher around the same time, penned "the greater the power the more dangerous the abuse". John Acton, historian and moralist, in 1887 added what is probably the best remembered, "power corrupts, absolute power corrupts absolutely. Great men are almost always bad men". While

Lincoln Steffens, an American editor and author in 1906 rounds off these quotes with "power is what men seek and any group that gets it will abuse it".

I am loath to get enthusiastic about any politician as the occupation requires people with a high regard of their own abilities. This usually means they are first and foremost about themselves and their careers, while the public good takes second place. Attending an election meeting addressed by Tony Blair in 1997, I was for once enthralled by his vision and presentation. He came across as a breath of fresh air to blow away the stifling stale layers of dust from previous regimes. Even with years of scepticism behind me, I was totally sold. One of my close friends, who had closer dealings with the Blair regime at the time, shook his head and foretold how disappointed I would become.

For the first months it did feel as if the cobwebs were in imminent danger of being blown away, but gradually the Iraq crisis began to show Blair's limited grasp of world affairs. No one who has read of the British governance of Iraq through the 1920s can be in any doubt that the country, with its three different tribes, was incapable of being administered other than by force. The British scuttled out of Iraq in 1932 at the end of their mandate, having been unable to bring lasting law and order to the country and it was only under the brutal regime of Saddam Hussein that the country could be governed.

This was so obvious that it remains a total mystery why our

Foreign Office failed to convince Blair of his idiocy in going along with the USA without UN authority. Iraq certainly turned out to be Blair's Charge of the Light Brigade, although perhaps worse, in that the charge was a mistake whereas Blair's decision was premeditated and the consequences unforgivable.

That Americans are not interested in history, only in making it, had already been demonstrated in Vietnam, so Blair was a slow learner. Indeed, it appears that neither George Bush nor Tony Blair had ever paused to study Confucius or they would have read more carefully his wise words – study the past if you would define the future. So on into Afghanistan while learning nothing from his predecessor, David Cameron then opens up a second front in Libya at the same time as drastically cutting back our Armed Forces. Self congratulation by NATO and its members on the success of the mission cannot mask the harsh fact that Cameron took a huge gamble by leading the support for a rebellion of unknown ability which could have led to serious consequences for us as a nation. When will we ever learn that grandiose gestures and being the world's policeman went out with Queen Victoria?

This episode has brought home to me the complexity of decision-making when our leaders are as liable as the rest of us to make stupid mistakes, but with far more serious consequences. I fear they may well repeat such folly in the future, as there is a distinct sense of lack of quality and resolve among the present generation of parliamentarians. Even our military leaders seem incapable of understanding the frailties of the human mind in adversity, appearing to expect civilians, such as the average poor Afghan, to ignore the terror of the Taliban and side with the forces of good when the outcome of the conflict appears so uncertain.

Personalities at war about their own futures, but played out on the national stage, was the Blair/Brown debacle. Of the two, Blair was a leader to encourage while Brown was a figure who inspired fear rather than hope. A typical product of a Scottish manse, Brown is in the mould of John Knox rather than an insightful, caring human being. Yet one of his priorities was relieving the suffering of the overseas poor, so highlighting the difficulty of pigeon holing individuals. A dark, overbearing presence, uncertain and diffident in office, he was an academic on the wrong road of life. Two such different people controlling the direction, hopes and fears of a whole nation is so sad in a modern free society, but there seems no practical answer to such human strength and weakness governing our destiny.

So are we in Scotland any better served in Holyrood? Westminster's lack of quality appears to be mirrored in our expensive new parliament. Bringing the decision-making closer to the people is certainly a promising initiative as long as our elected MSPs are more capable than our distant masters in London. The May 2011 elections showed the Scottish Tory Party and Liberal Democrats in total disarray and Labour unable to hold on to its traditional seats, so we now have a very unbalanced representation dealing with our problems.

The Scottish National Party, sincere in its beliefs, is in fact the nigger in the wood pile for Scottish and UK politics. It sits like a time bomb, obvious to all, but no one knows exactly how it is primed. Waiting for the economy to improve looks like giving us a breather from its threat, but in the meantime Scottish politics is in limbo. Nothing can be planned with certainty until we know the status of Scotland in the future. As Scots we are pulled two ways – national pride would like us to be a country in our own right, while hard-headedness makes us wonder if our grandchildren could find themselves second class citizens in these islands in the future.

The recent collapse of our Scottish world leading banks, the gradual run down of the oil reserves off our coast, as well as the massive loss of the old industries of coal and ship building, suggest we should be practical and stick with the larger UK economy. This is particularly true with the public sector in Scotland being so large and top heavy compared with England. Common sense should be telling us all that the UK economy is bad enough, but Scotland on its own could in time find itself looking south for help and that would be totally demoralising.

At present Alec Salmond and some of his ministers appear as probably the best of a poor lot looking after our affairs. Despite recent SNP successes the Scottish population is still probably unconvinced regarding a separate state and now looking at Iceland and the Irish Republic it appears our fears are well founded. However, there is a strong nationalistic fervour among many Scots which would rather see Scotland sink below the waves than belong to a UK where England is the dominant partner.

Now with a top heavy SNP representation we can expect the steady subtle manipulation of public opinion to view a separate state as a reasonable alternative. Already the political tone has changed to one of hectoring demands and projecting the image of victimisation, which augurs for conflict with central government for the next few years, so it will be interesting to see how effective this proves in changing public sentiment.

Scotland for generations has been an exporter of its talents so has this had a positive or negative outcome for us in our northern retreat? I am always astonished at the Scottish accents that come across in the media in every sector of life south of the border. Westminster has been dominated by Scots; the medical profession was called the Scottish mafia in my time, so why are we so bothered about nationhood when we almost run the UK. Surely it is better to play in the Premier League for Arsenal than for the likes of Gordon Brown's Raith Rovers.

I have moved only 20 miles from home to carry out my life's work, but I well recognise that we stay-at-homers are not the pioneers who have made Scots renowned throughout the world. I firmly believe Scots have a far greater future playing on the UK stage than relegated to a miniscule part in world affairs.

However, while this mirage of Utopia is dangled, hearts will rule and canny heads will be ignored.

Another marker for those keen to see a separate Scotland is to look at our local authorities. Aberdeen has seen billions of dollars worth of oil extracted on its doorstep, but such is the incompetence of our local leaders that the infrastructure has been ignored and our transport is grinding to a gridlock. Decisions have been deferred and deferred in so many quarters that now with financial hardship upon us, the time has passed for radical measures. Private enterprise has luckily boomed for Aberdeen, but in a vacuum of public enterprise. Shetland showed how to collar some of the oil money for its residents' benefit, whereas our North-East has totally failed. Similarly the local authority in Edinburgh, with its prestigious tram system, has demonstrated just how not to get things done. This does not augur much encouragement for a separate Scotland, while the crowning incompetence was the Scottish parliament building, predicted to cost no more than £40 million and ending up at the staggering figure of £414 million. Ten times over budget and we look to run our own affairs?

I, however, remain immensely proud to be Scottish, British and with an envious eye to the French when they play their rugby with flair and flourish. I believe we often fail to appreciate how lucky we are to live in such a free country despite so many drawbacks, which we seem to always stress rather than the strengths.

Abroad, despite my name, I always insist I am a Scot, usually accompanied with some disparaging remark about our English neighbours. From my point of view it is tongue in cheek to draw attention to my background, but it does show that some of us do carry a chip on our shoulders. I recognise that this differentiation between our home nations is completely arbitrary, as populations have intermingled throughout the generations, so making most of us a hotch-potch of tribes.

For the average Scot to rage on about the English, whether on the sports field or reacting to English people settling in their area, is small minded and ignorant of history. However the seeds of discontent are as much due to our southern neighbour, with its past and present arrogant disregard for Scottish sensitivities.

The United Kingdom's union flag and national anthem are the outcome of a shared heritage and a demonstration of national unity and pride. For any one home country, therefore, to claim the right to use it to distinguish it from their fellow citizens is bizarre. Yet the Rugby Six Nations has England using our nation's national anthem as its own trademark. This is unbelievable arrogance, but highlights the stupidity of the officials of Scotland, Wales and Northern Ireland for condoning such a divisive decision. Similarly with soccer, Welsh supporters seen recently booing the National Anthem inflamed supporters and players alike with their senseless bigotry. Such imagery spreads far further than the games of rugby or football to the detriment of our sense of national unity and plays into those advocating the end of the Union. Perhaps the saddest aspect of all this is that sport's followers of our home nations accept this debasement without a murmur, yet again showing that 90 percent of us are fairly unthinking.

As regards public opinion, we often hear politicians or interested parties clamouring to take notice of this when they are trying to achieve some aim. Public opinion, however, is frequently a sham. For the public to have any meaningful input, it must first have a clear understanding of all the facts. The furore over the lack of a referendum regarding membership of the European Union is an outstanding example. The popular assumption is that a vote at present would get a resounding NO, but the public appears ignorant of the pros and cons.

Whether men or women are running a golf club or a mighty organisation like the EU, they bring similar strengths and weaknesses. A golf club in the wrong hands loses sight of its primary function and can spend money needlessly, hire excessive staff, all at a cost to members who see no benefit to their own game of golf. Members properly informed, however, can get involved and vote for change or choose to resign. If the nearest golf club is thirty miles away this decision is not to be taken too lightly. Similarly with the EU; it has become a gigantic bureaucratic empire growing out of control. Sadly, the UK is not economically strong enough to ignore any potential benefits which may accrue from belonging to such a club, no matter how indifferently it is run. The alternative is to go it alone, but in cut-throat world markets this would be no hazard-free option. The judgement over whether to stay and work to improve the system or leave is finely balanced depending on whether the benefits outweigh the losses or vice versa. At present the electorate has no evidence either way, so any decision would be made in abject ignorance - a salutary example of the nonsense of public opinion.

Yes, the years of innocence disappear all too quickly in our lives, but it does pay in the long run not to believe everything you read, nor yet what politicians may say. For example, Tony Blair walks off into his prosperous Westminster sunset sidling into the Catholic Church along the way, but regretting nothing, with half a million dead Iraqis behind him. A brilliant actor and politician, but behind the façade just another mere mortal depending on mysticism to justify his certainties in life. World powers promote him to become their Middle East special envoy, despite the fact the he has done so much to destabilise this whole area; even his writings show he is not without bias.

So what is the future for Britain in this 21st century with little sign of any dynamic leadership to take us out of our present crisis? Have 400 years of being a prominent world nation instilled anything into our genes to make us survivors? We have had an uncanny knack of muddling through and overcoming tragedies like Dunkirk, always coming back fighting, so can we depend on this stubborn streak in the future?

Through the ages we have produced so many innovative

thinkers and doers to keep us in the van of progress, with not a little help from our immigrant groups. For countless generations, way before Roman times, we have opposed or welcomed foreigners to these shores, but almost without exception they have been the very people to assist in inserting the word 'great' into our vocabulary.

Jews and Europeans, often fleeing persecution, have been at the forefront of our Empire with not a few Scots leaving their homeland to stamp our authority around the globe. It seems that scarcely a prominent figure in our society has not some genetic link, from the recent past or present, to a foreign country, yet the average British citizen is emotionally opposed to this continuing inflow of immigrants gradually changing us to a multi-colour state.

The inflow of Asians has brought a fresh perspective to our business and computing industries, while the West Indians and others bring their own particular skills and personalities. True, many incomers fleeing adversity or being economic migrants may not initially add to the wealth of the country, but this has to be carefully balanced by the huge potential benefits from people that have had the initiative to leave their own countries to hazard their futures in an alien environment. Like adding fresh blood strains to improve cattle or horse breeding stock, so the introduction of new active ambitious human genes into an island community has had the UK performing far beyond what such a population would normally achieve.

The dilemma for any government is to balance benefit against resources to cope with the inflow. The disappointing fact has to be faced that we have a significant core of indolent, native-born inhabitants not prepared to work, being a drain on the shared wealth of us all and with a lifestyle that almost ensures their offspring will follow the route of their parents.

There is a drive to identify the genuinely unfit and those abusing the system. However, with my years of experience assessing such claimants, a doctor may correctly pass someone fit for work, but then reality kicks in. How do you find anyone, especially in the private sector, misguided enough to employ a person who feels victimised and continues to insist on his/her unfitness. At a time when some of our keenest toil to find suitable occupations, what hope is there for those not similarly motivated, while being substantially cushioned by state largesse? A baffling set of problems which will stretch the ingenuity and patience of many future governments, as well as society in general.

CLASS, PERSONALITY AND BIZARRE BEHAVIOUR

"OUR OBJECT IN THE CONSTRUCTION OF THE STATE IS THE GREATEST HAPPINESS OF THE WHOLE AND NOT THAT OF ANY ONE CLASS"

PLATO
Greek Philosopher and Mathematician
circa 400BC

There is a popular perception in modern day Britain that social class no longer is of any great importance. Such remarks frequently emanate from politicians across all parties. Looking at the present mother of parliaments it does seem that Eton, Oxford and Cambridge ride high in the offices of state, while other public schools are well represented throughout, but whether this is now considered worthy of comment is uncertain.

As a native of this country, but only coming into contact with a restricted cross-section of society, it is difficult to assess if class plays any part, in not only our everyday lives, but how we are governed locally and nationally. I have an interesting outsider source of perception, as my daughter, having been an Australian resident for the past twenty years, gives me her comments and assessments on regular trips home.

From my childhood days in the 1930s I have lived in this North-East corner of Scotland all my life, other than two years of National Service, but still consider myself world travelled. The changes over this period have been momentous and all the obvious indicators of serfdom have disappeared. The abuses and misuses of the poor, such as agricultural workers and the widespread servant class have passed, but servile attitudes to ones perceived betters still exist widely below the surface

The cloth-capped thousands who flocked to Hampden Park are no more with the fading away of the heavy industries of mining and ship building, so the sense of a homogeneous working class has ceased to exist. Ask people how they now see themselves and middle class seems the most common.

Certainly the booming oil industry has changed the face of North-East Scotland, with a level of wealth spread through society which would have been unthinkable 60 years ago.

Yet deep demarcations still exist, as sociologists are quick to point out. Even with its oil wealth, a survey of Aberdeen some years ago of the social pecking order by occupation still rated academics first with the top professions second, while the business and oil sectors were further down the scale. This was surprising as one would expect that the wealth of oil would elevate it past the traditional occupations, but old values persist. In the early days, around 1972, the first American oil pioneers confidently informed me Aberdeen would be transformed into a Houston within twenty years and that oil wealth would dominate the scene. Into the second decade of a new century the old city of Aberdeen has indeed changed, not always for the better, but still remains true to its centuries-old roots. Perhaps it is down to the fact that this part of the world doesn't much like flaunted wealth, and its enthusiasm for things new takes a generation or two to become established.

The transformation of the city's hinterland is for me the biggest change. Where farms and steadings were gradually crumbling, they are now mostly converted to up-market dwellings with at least one 4x4 by the front door. Private education booms, while in the recreational sector outdoor pursuits such as shooting syndicates are now made up of a cross-section of workers, mainly in oil, displacing the more snobby gatherings of the old moneyed class and stuffy professions. At this level class distinction has certainly disappeared, and even select golf clubs have had to come to terms with the fact that status and recommendation are no longer the main criteria; if they are to remain solvent, money must dominate.

My daughter, leaving the laid back, almost classless Antipodes for her regular visit home, feels she returns straight into a society riddled with class. Old friends greet her with talk of their big houses, important husbands, luxury holidays and high achieving children. The need not to be left behind in the rat-race requires a new Mercedes to keep pace with the neighbours, the discovery of the latest fabulous ski resort or flashy new restaurant. A set of values alien to her new homeland, which she admits could benefit from a little more interest in education, but not to the extent of a society driven by prestige and peer group pressures.

So what of personality? Can man move on from his inherited conventional thinking and attitudes? Personality is divided by the academics into five categories: Openness, Conscientiousness, Extraversion, Agreeableness and Neuroticism.

'Openness' distinguishes the imaginative from the conventional. Open to experience, new ideas and intellectually curious, they are appreciative of art and sensitive to beauty. Compared with closed people, they are more creative and more aware of their own feelings. They are also more likely to hold unconventional beliefs.

'Conscientiousness' is the tendency to show self-discipline and act dutifully with a preference for planned rather than spontaneous behaviour. It influences the way in which we control, regulate and direct our impulses and contains the factor known as NAch (Need for Achievement).

'Extraversion' is characterised by positive emotions and a tendency to seek out stimulation and the company of others. Marked engagement with the outside world, action-oriented and often seen as full of energy. Introverts lack social exuberance, preferring to be low key, but may still be energetic, simply not socially.

'Agreeableness' is a tendency to be compassionate and cooperative, rather than suspicious and antagonistic towards others. A desire to get along and willing to compromise their interests for harmony is a strong characteristic. Disagreeable people place self-interest above getting on with others, while being sceptical about others motives makes them appear suspicious, unfriendly and uncooperative.

'Neuroticism' is the tendency to show negative emotions such as anger, anxiety or depression and is sometimes termed emotional instability. Such people are more likely to interpret ordinary situations as threatening and minor frustrations as hopelessly difficult, while being very vulnerable to stress. Their mood tends to be labile, undermining their ability to think clearly, make decisions and cope effectively with their tensions.

With such a wide range of options we feel that we can place ourselves fairly accurately somewhere in each category. However, it appears that what we are comes from generations past and our choice for change is all too limited. True, we can become aware of our worst traits and try to amend them, but it needs insight, understanding, intelligence and a real purpose to make an appreciable difference to personality.

Unfortunately neuroticism is unlikely to be altered by greater insight, while severe introverts could never see themselves as the swingers of society. Certainly most of us could be a lot more agreeable and looking out for others is a message which should resonate with us all. Yes, some things can be improved but sadly no mountains can be moved to make man more sensible or change much in society.

Personality stereotyping is followed by the two sciences – behavioural and social – to complete our ability to cope with our environment, making it a miracle that some of us can climb out of bed in a morning. Fortunately, few recognise that such measures exist so are saved the thankless business of regular self assessment. Some events which happen in our everyday lives, however, cause us to try to fathom why they occurred, though the clues were always there for us to read.

My star Radio 4 programme is *Today* with John Humphrys and James Naughtie, which always starts my day with a bang. There is no greater gap for me with weeks away in Australia or on some more exotic adventure than missing those well kent voices which reassure me that we are living in a worthwhile nation. Many find the interview techniques of Humphrys and Paxman beyond the bounds of decency and fairness, but I find their approach refreshing in a society where all too few are prepared to tackle our devious and often vacuous masters head on.

Professor Anthony Clare's *In the Psychiatrist's Chair* used to follow *Today* on a weekday, and was also compulsive listening. One particular interview remained imprinted on my brain as evidence of how some can reach positions of power despite their obvious flaws. Miss Ann Widdecombe born in 1947 was an MP from 1987 until retiring in 2010. She held the post of Minister of State for Prisons in the Major government when she is remembered for backing a policy of shackling pregnant women with handcuffs and chains right up to delivery, while in contrast being avidly anti fox hunting. She held shadow posts, including Home Secretary, for a short time after Blair ousted the Tories in 1997. A novelist since then and a convert to Catholicism mainly over the ordination of women, she is well known for her direct approach and sharp wit, making journalists wary of upsetting her.

The interview in June 1997 was riveting as the suave, gently-probing Clare ran into an impenetrable stone wall, with Widdecombe taking the conversation only where she wanted it without compromise. It became very clear that Miss Widdecombe had ideas and views on everything which were inviolate and she would not brook that she could possibly be wrong. Her performance was later described as "dogma personified" as well as "totally arrogant". It certainly was dogma of the most extreme kind, which included her extreme religious beliefs for all to sample.

Little did I think she would once more appear to startle us all, but in 2010 the BBC recruited her to appear on *Strictly Come Dancing*, a spectacular show which attracted millions of viewers. But why would they recruit a lady of her years and doubtful shape in the company of so many talented people? Her dancing ability was truly dreadful, although her determination and physical endeavour were to be admired. Viewers voting on her performance kept her on the show for weeks, giving the BBC a suitable riposte for its arrogance in such a blatant use of an ugly duckling to promote viewing numbers.

The question of whether this was exploitation by the BBC of a person with limited insight raises difficult moral questions, as does an episode on the reality TV show *Big Brother*. The Respect politician George Galloway acting a pussycat being sensually fed by a fellow participant must plumb the depths of demeaning behaviour, which even Miss Widdecombe could not reach. Both showed a frightening level of public self-debasement by elected politicians. Two substantial political figures, incapable of perceiving themselves as appearing ridiculous, is truly startling; one even holding the post of shadow Home Secretary, a post of significance even in opposition.

Suddenly we realise that power could so worryingly land up in the hands of dogmatists and blinkered exhibitionists. There is also a serious question mark against the insight of those who promoted them, especially the lady.

Predictably another large political ego, Edwina Currie – Health Minister in 1988 who was forced to resign after maintaining that most of Britain's egg production was infected with salmonella bacteria – cannot resist keeping herself in the public eye by following Miss Widdecombe on to *Strictly Come Dancing*.

So where does Mrs Thatcher fit into this picture with her direct and confident approach? Did she ever exhibit much insight into herself? The nagging feeling persists that she was not much interested in intellectual self-examination and tended to follow her own inclinations. Her success as a true lioness of our age is recognised, but with too much 'Openness' of personality would she have achieved so much? Personality checking does not always mean there is a right attribute as against a wrong one. There is little doubt, however, that Lady T, as she was to become, would have told the BBC in no uncertain terms where to put their invitation to appear on their glitzy *Come Dancing*.

A View from the Foothills is the political diaries of Chris Mullin, a minister in the Blair government from 1992 to 2005, which open up a world of political life which is intriguing but deeply depressing. Personality and behaviour bringing out all the baser elements of man's nature, mixed up with flashes of decency, confirming all the public's doubts about our elected representatives and also the slump in Civil Service standards. It gives us, too, an insight into the living conditions and behaviour in the lower elements of society from Mullin's experience as Labour MP for Sunderland South. The hopelessness of those existing on such bleak housing estates brings home the sense that we are caught in an ever-widening set of circumstances outwith the ability of our leaders to tackle, and with all too much liable to fall on the willing in the voluntary sector.

Meanwhile money and the public schools have done an excellent job, if not in changing personalities, then certainly hiding them from public gaze. Prominent figures like David Cameron and his Chancellor George Osborne regularly appear before us, yet their impenetrable façades leave us uncertain of who they are or what they really believe in. Are they genuinely men of the people giving their all for the nation, or are they quietly self-interested, doing it all for personal satisfaction? We, the plebs, will probably never know, but then that has always been the way, so nothing has changed.

Finally, having spent the last 30 years expounding, through articles, letters to the press and personal contacts, my abiding dislike of our class system, I have to recognise that I am just not winning. The message bounces off my fellow citizens like rain off a taut umbrella, draining away totally without trace. I realise that the system is so inbuilt that few see it as of any moment in their lives. Both the superior and serf-like attitudes in the strata of society are so drilled into the British way of life that some misguided hero-worshippers even appear unwittingly prepared to extend rather than curtail them.

Only occasionally do I feel my message of continuing inequality has hit a sensitive nerve when recipients of the various doled out honours appear almost shamefaced when I meet them. Not that my opinion counts for anything, but within themselves I am sure that the insightful are far less certain of the merits of the system than their apparent public delight merits. Man is what he has always been; a member of the pack owing allegiance to whoever is most dominant and influential at the time and only too happy to accept what trifles fall from that all-powerful table.

Unsettlingly, I have to admit that offered such an honour I too might struggle to put principle before self-aggrandisement. No one would applaud my sacrifice, but would readily pay lip service to my honour, so where would the spun coin settle – heads or tails? Luckily, with my public views so well known, I shall never experience the temptation to test whether I am a man or a mouse, thank goodness.

THOUGHTS ON
THE END OF LIFE

"I AM NOT AFRAID OF DEATH; I JUST DON'T
WANT TO BE THERE WHEN IT HAPPENS"

WOODY ALLEN

Both my parents enjoyed really long lives, both dying in their
98th year. There is little doubt that being born with the right
genes is a huge benefit both to health and longevity. In France
my last cousin died in her 102nd year and a host of others have
lasted into their nineties.

Does this mean that I welcome the thought of living a
further 10 years or more? Unhappily it does not, as I watched

my father become gradually more and more enfeebled. Macular degeneration of his sight meant increasing blindness so that his love of reading was denied him. His detailed interest in his garden became a thing of the past, while his daily walk became shorter by the month. Both parents coming to live with our family saw him swiftly become more loath to move around and then one day he accused my mother of trying to poison him.

Over the months this became a regular theme and he showed his desperation by asking the postman one day to get a doctor quickly, as he was sure he was being slowly killed. The stress on my mother and spreading throughout the household was worrying as he had been such a pleasant, stoical man all his life. Seeking a break for my mother's sake, we managed to arrange for him to go into the local cottage hospital for a month. Two days later he slipped on their wooden floor and fractured his hip. Hip pinned, he had great difficulty in finding his balance on standing and was moved to a long stay bed for physiotherapy.

Weeks passed as he lay not quite sure whether it was night or day and my regular vigil at his bedside was a dreadfully unhappy experience. Finally, sent out to the cottage hospital where he had broken his leg, he rapidly developed pneumonia. Still fighting to the end, our last visit saw him semi-conscious and gasping for breath. Yet in the midst of his misery he still insisted on struggling to sit up to pass urine. Right to the very end he would not allow standards to slip. Two days later he passed away, all on his own, as I was at work and ever since I have looked back and felt I deserted him at the last.

My mother entered an old folk's home some years later as she felt she had become a burden to the household, but lived for another five years. Independent of mind, she found her fellow residents old and uninteresting, although she was by far the oldest, so she elected to spend most of her life in her own room. Failing eyesight and general weakness did not stop her from welcoming stimulating visitors and she would come alive with reminiscences and political argument. She detested Margaret Thatcher and nothing would rouse her more surely than any reference to the Iron Lady.

She just faded away one night in 1989 the nurses checked to settle her down and half an hour later going in to see that she was okay found that she had departed to meet her maker, as she had prayed to do so for many years. Her quality of life in her latter years was nil, just as my father's had been, so is there a conclusion to draw?

I loved both my parents very dearly and dreaded the day I would lose them. Yet both outlived what I would have wished for them, as the last few years held nothing but tedium for my mother and an increasing mental obsession and fear for my father.

I highlight their latter years to consider the vexed question of assisted suicide – a description I do not like, much preferring assisted dying. Throughout my years as a doctor I have been at times in a position to assist in terminating life, but not once have I wittingly done so. The reason for this is much more complex than many doctors admit and which those advocating changing the law seem loath to seriously consider.

As a young doctor I was always far more interested in perpetuating life rather than thinking of ending it. Once or twice I hauled patients back from the brink with a battery of treatments, but it quickly dawned on me that my heroics often led to the patient having a far nastier death than if I had left them to slip away. My final lesson in this field was with a delightful old man with diabetes. My having looked after him for many years, he became very feeble, went off his feet and stopped eating. When he developed pneumonia I launched in with powerful antibiotics and against the odds he began to improve. For a week I felt very satisfied until on my regular check I noticed he had developed gangrene in the toes of one foot. Admitted to hospital he had an above knee amputation and eventually returned home, a shadow of his former self, to die in some distress a few weeks later. In retrospect, I realised I had brought nothing but pain and anxiety, not only to the patient, but also to his wife. I had learnt a stern lesson.

Over my career many patients died at home and although I gave them adequate pain relief, this was never to the point of knowingly hastening their end. In a hospice where many patients are admitted to get monitored pain relief due to their terminal condition, I am in no doubt that in the final hours drugs may just hasten the end. For me, this is quite different from the patient at home, as I had enough experience to know that patients' relatives at times have a knack of putting two and two together, not always to your benefit. To be told by a neighbour that the doctor came and gave the patient an injection and of course death occurred within the hour is extremely worrying, especially with litigation now so prevalent. Such rumours, especially in small communities, spread quickly, so doctors become very defensive, making sure that such rumours can never start. Occasionally I felt I could have assisted dying to terminate suffering, but self preservation made it a risk too far, which is really sad.

I always remember my mother telling me that my grandmother had been given the 'blue pill' from her doctor when she was dying. Mother firmly believed that the doctor had killed her and that it was common knowledge that this was a standard practice in those days of the 1930s. The blue pill, according to records, contained a high level of mercury and was used for various illnesses, including depression, but there is no word of its use in the terminally ill. Whatever its use in my grandmother's case, as far as popular belief went, it was to kill, so I was always wary not to become associated with such dying.

At present the battle rages over whether those assisting a patient to die are breaking the law and liable to be prosecuted. Both in Scotland and Westminster the tussle goes on to introduce a more enlightened set of regulations. The bizarre situation is that suicide was decriminalised here in 1961, but it appears a crime has been committed by those assisting or associated with a suicide, while the suicide itself is not a crime. Meanwhile, different countries with different laws can see British patients going to a clinic on the continent to have lethal drugs administered to terminate life. Those accompanying them are seen as accomplices and on returning to the UK can be questioned by the police and in theory brought to court and sentenced for up to 14 years in prison.

Looking at this problem compassionately, if the patient has reached his/her decision that life has become unbearable, it seems inhumane not to allow those who are dearest to them to be in attendance. If it is clear that no pressure has been brought on the patient to make such a decision, then the law should accommodate such action. However, it is when the activists wish to broaden the approach that I begin to have reservations.

At present throughout the world there are four areas where euthanasia or assisted suicide is practised: Oregon, Belgium, Netherlands and Switzerland. In the first three, two doctors and if necessary a psychologist are required to obtain the necessary go-ahead, whereas in Switzerland only one doctor is involved, although the reasons for assisting must be altruistic as the law requires. The only country offering the service to foreigners at present is Switzerland and it has been inundated with requests from all over the world. Only one of the four registered clinics, Dignitas, offers the service to outsiders, so all the pressure has descended on that one company. The criteria are rigid and include that the patient must be terminally or severely mentally ill, or clinically depressed beyond treatment. Patients are provided with counselling and then treatment with lethal drugs.

Should we in this country move to the Swiss situation and face reality? It is certainly unsatisfactory for patients in dire distress to have the added burden of finding an overseas clinic, with the spectre of their relatives returning home to face prosecution. Yet there is something unsettling about the taking of human life, no matter the circumstances and I find it an uncomfortable area to discuss.

I can understand the need for the fullest discussion. A bill, brought by MSP Margo MacDonald, who herself suffers from Parkinson's disease, was before the Scottish Parliament only to be eventually heavily defeated. The bill set out that the terminally ill be able to ask willing doctors to help them die at a time of their choosing. My reservations are not in the principle, but in the process.

Some of my unhappiest memories from General Practice were in the field of human relationships surrounding the dying. Elderly spinsters or widows who had never seen a relative for 20 years began to fail in health and with the end in sight, odd cousins, nieces, etc., would appear on the scene from all over the country. What I came to recognise as 'the Sunday visit syndrome' repeated itself in one form or another far too often to sustain my belief in human nature.

Sunday afternoon on weekend duty, the phone would ring and this would be a niece from London who just happened to be in the district and had called in to see her aunt. Quite distressed to find her so poorly, she wished an immediate home visit to get her into a home or hospital – anywhere – but something had to be done NOW. My West End practice was populated by many rich elderly patients and I was immediately suspicious that pound signs were flashing in front of a concerned relative. It seems cynical to relate concern for others in the same breath as personal gain, but so many people played this game of inveigling themselves into the dying patient's good books that it was difficult to distinguish the genuine from the carpet baggers.

My deep concern about assisted dying lies in exactly this area of personal gain. We show our true colours when we stop speaking to our sister or brother when someone inherits that Chinese vase we fancied, or those mock Sheraton chairs in our parent's will. For every one person who refuses to get into this family squabble, there seem at least two who have no such scruples. We are all influenced by those around us and it is quite simple to visualise cases where insidious pressure could be brought on the terminally ill to hasten the process.

We bandy about terms like terminally ill which can be very imprecise. All we need is to recall the case of the so-called Libyan bomber Al Megrahi, who was given three months to live and was still alive over a year later. Physicians had given what they believed was an average assessment for such an illness, but it turned out to be wildly pessimistic. I learnt, with years of experience, that every person responds differently to such illnesses and we as doctors just made fools of ourselves to predict. Patients and relatives expected accuracy, which it is impossible for us to supply. Also the environment the patient is in helps or hinders depending whether it is all gloom and doom, or cheerful and positive.

The medical profession is amazingly imprecise at times as to what it considers terminal, especially related to depressive illness, with doctor differing from doctor. The term the 'willing doctor' in Margo MacDonald's bill raises the question: what defines 'a willing doctor'. Without casting aspersions at my profession, the word willing can have more than one meaning and I am sure I might not be too happy to be assessed by some.

The cases of Bodkin Adams and Harold Shipman show how these doctors got away with murder for years under the very noses of relatives and other doctors. While these were extreme cases, there is little doubt that other more minor cases exist and in practice I always knew the doctors I had to double check with before, for instance, signing the second part of their cremation forms.

Altruistic initiatives are to be welcomed as long as we remember that human beings do not always live up to such high ideals. It is far better to plan for the weaknesses than ignore them and hope common decency will prevail.

So at the end of the day would any of this thinking have affected my outlook on the death of my parents, or for that matter myself or my family in due course? My father died in horrible circumstances – gasping for breath, but conscious enough to try keep his dignity. In a hospice he would have been assisted in dying, perhaps three days beforehand, which would have been a humane outcome.

My mother, still mentally alert, just slipped away after gradually becoming weaker, but not really suffering. I have always felt her death was so peaceful that assisted dying would never have arisen. Her quality of life beforehand was extremely poor, but medically there was no reason to assist her in dying, although she repeatedly stated she wished it. She believed she was going to heaven and for months before her death prayed every night to God to take her. Given some relative encouraging her, could she have then asked a 'willing doctor' to assist her dying prematurely? This is a real worry; once a regulation is formulated, it must be watertight or some will surely abuse it.

As for myself, I hugely value life and do not look forward to going through the process of dying. At the end, however, I would never like my family to see me suffer as I saw my father. So, yes, at the end do not resuscitate me and make sure I slip away quietly, just like my mother.

Let me not end on a sad note, but allow me to salute all those who have given their lives to others to make sure that suffering is kept to the minimum. They so often go beyond the bounds of duty in their caring. Apart from a handful of abuses I witnessed in practice, the honest endeavour of the great majority was something I always admired.

THE NEED FOR HUMOUR

"HUMOUR IS MANKIND'S GREATEST BLESSING"

MARK TWAIN (1835-1910)
American Author and Humorist

I am acutely aware that throughout these pages there is a distinct lack of light-heartedness as I struggle with the mysticism of the past and the incongruities of today. Before closing these chapters, therefore, I shall pause and look at how the human mind combats some of the intricacies of every day living.

The North-East of Scotland has not only its very own

characteristic Doric dialect, but along with it a very droll, dry sense of humour. It is said of the troops in World War I that the local lads who went to fight from this part of Britain made excellent soldiers. They expected nothing but hardship from their own upbringing, while a stoical sense of humour made light of adversity, with the ever repeated expression that everything was "nae bad". Stoical to the point of foolhardiness, they would, like so many others of that generation, walk to certain death across no-man's-land as they were just obeying orders, and no one disobeyed orders.

Brought up in the country district of Deeside in Aberdeenshire and first attending a small two-teacher school, I rapidly learnt this culture; never show fear, never show emotion, never show too much enthusiasm for anything and you might just be tolerated. Coming from a home of sophisticated comfort and with parents who were far removed from this type of thinking, this descended on me like an icy cold shower.

Probably over protected and rather spoilt as a late only child, the difference from my background and this basic way of thinking and acting took me many months to get used to. In addition my name caused cruel humour and banter among my schoolmates and undue attention from my teachers.

I look back on the experience as trying, but character forming and throughout life it has certainly done me no harm. Getting used to being called Froggie Fouin and being accused of eating frog's legs for dinner soon thickened the skin. I must have had some bad times, however, as I can distinctly remember my mother repeating again and again that "sticks and stones will break your bones, but names will never hurt you".

Being blessed with a fairly unruffled temperament and not easily inflamed to anger, I have rarely felt the need to resort to fisticuffs. Never having had to fight my corner with siblings, I have never knowingly been in a physical scrap of anger in my life. I am sure this is exceptional for a boy, but it does have a downside. Not having faced much physical violence, how, I wonder would I react? I know exactly the state of my moral courage, but my physical side, even today, remains untested.

Developing an acute sense, from my earliest school days, when physical trouble could be brewing, I became adept at either making myself scarce, or positioning myself to snuff out the problem before it unfolded. This often involved the use of rough, badgering humour which could deflate some bullies. Chaffing the bully and even appearing to counter his physical approach before he was ready, needed confidence, but as with all such experiences regular refinement meant ever more effectiveness. My general approach to life must have been quite peaceable, as I was rarely at loggerheads with any of my mates, although I was never a very passive member of anything I joined.

Throughout my later school days and at university I found that the bantering, pulling the leg type of humour best suited my temperament. Deflating serious discussion by a ribald comment, I found could make opponents into friends, although both sides still fought their corner. It was obvious that if insulting friends and foes alike was light-hearted and not malicious, others would respond in kind, so developing a sense of camaraderie even with the opposition.

In my early professional life I found this approach just did not work on some of my seniors who saw no humour in this young upstart's remarks. Used to being feted and looked up to, any suggestion of a little mickey-taking was an unforgivable insult. Under these conditions I found my own sense of humour deserting me and the fight almost became so personal that actual dislike reared its head for the only time in my life.

Happily those years passed quickly; gradually, with a level of acceptance among colleagues, the sense of humour and camaraderie returned. In my practice work I found that humour and ability to laugh at ourselves is a huge asset. Always prepared to see the positive side of things and treat each patient as an important individual, I tried to add a little humour wherever possible. Patients became so used to this approach and responded so readily to it, that when I was in a more sober mind they would ask if I was well enough.

Every patient responds differently and a one club approach suits all has no place. As the doctor listens for the tell-tale remark that gives an insight to the patient's needs, so it is with humour. I have at times badly miscued my approach when, ignoring tell-tale signs, I have waded in with some silly remark.

Greeting a very glum patient with a cheery comment only to be told her husband died that morning is a lesson never to be forgotten. Back-tracking into concern is a poor response after such a *faux pas*. So it is with life in general – using humour is only relevant at certain times, while using it indiscriminately fingers you as insensitive and irresponsible.

The multi-racial mix of the UK is something we in the north of the country are only now becoming aware of. Many of us have over the years referred disparagingly to certain foreigners, which would have us in serious trouble in today's climate. A number of my university friends were from overseas and the banter between us was always friendly and light-hearted, with no one taking offence. This has all changed and even our favourite pastime of poking fun at our southern neighbour has become hazardous.

Having retired, I still carried out medical boards on the disabled and we were occasionally vetted from Edinburgh to ensure that we were up to standard. At one of these sessions one of my colleagues, referring to a claimant from south of the border who seemed to be making a trivial claim, light-heartedly commented that of course he was English, so what could you expect. A typical throw-away remark among colleagues, only good enough for a snigger, especially with English friends present. The vetting doctor – a local Scot – reported it back to Edinburgh, however, and my colleague was warned if this occurred again he would be dismissed. They say the law can be an ass, but in my opinion it is usually those who enforce it, using no common sense, who are the guilty parties. In the backwaters of retirement we still poke fun at each other, especially if Yorkshiremen are around; then the insults fly with no holds barred, thoroughly enjoyed by all.

Banter and leg-pulling form the basis of our humour in the UK and it can often be more cruel than funny. This was brought home forcibly when I had a German student from Bremen seconded to me over twenty-five years ago. He had been on an exchange with Exeter and had been hurt by what he had seen and experienced in contact with students and lecturers alike. He dismissed the banter as not being humour, as someone was always the butt of the so-called jokes. He thought it all crude, hurtful and insensitive. He found the same type of humour among the Scots, but said it was always accompanied with a smile and a sense of bonhomie. I appreciated his tact, but from my own experience I think he was being rather too kind to us.

My daughter, married to an Australian doctor, has opened another avenue where humour has an important part to play. My memory of Australian doctors goes back to the late 1950s in the Aberdeen Maternity Hospital. That doyen of medicine, Prof. Sir Dugald Baird, ruled the roost in Aberdeen with his worldwide reputation, but the Aussies were not phased one little bit by such trappings. Baird had himself brought these Aussies to Aberdeen to train, but they showed no inferiority complex by regularly challenging Sir Dugald, in all our meetings, to justify his comments. We sat around totally gobsmacked, as no home-trained medic would dare to challenge the great man. To give Sir Dugald his due he seemed to revel in the combat, with not a little of his Glaswegian sense of humour breaking through. Moreover he always appeared to pay more attention to the comments from Oz that he did to those of the subservient locals.

Now with twenty years of regularly visiting Australia I find my sense of humour, honed in the Glen Tanar playground, is ideal for dealing with these pushy Australians. Leave an Aussie alone and he will rapidly make an idiot of you with all his humour based around his convict ancestry and kicking the Poms. Although this term may relate to anyone from the home countries, Scots prefer to think of Poms as English.

Having established you are not a Sassenach, you must then carry the fight directly to them with the grossest insults you can think up. They just love it, recognising a fellow human being giving back as good as they get. You never seem to be able to really insult them and they lap it all up with good grace.

Still a country built on the culture around all being mates, there is something wonderfully refreshing to see how they unstintingly help one another without any thought of reimbursement. I am a huge fan of the Australians, but get a massive kick out of seeing the old country put one over them in the sporting arena just once in a while.

Yes, humour is such an important component of life and yet we all seem programmed to appreciate it in different ways. I love the couthy humour of the North-East based around its rural background. Stories surrounding gruff old farmers with their lack of emotion or playing down adversity to a ridiculous level, always raises hoots of laughter. The fact that it is so close to the truth makes it so much more hilarious. For me this is real humour as exemplified by that wonderful trio of Steve Robertson, Buff Hardie and George Donald who made up Scotland the What? until a few years ago. For me the slapstick humour of the United States scarcely raises a smile, but Steve acting Bruce's Spider has me rolling in the aisles.

My time doing National Service gave me enough of an insight into the Armed Forces to know that humour is one of the main constituents that mould units into a cohesive force. True, it may not always be in the best of taste, nor sensitive as to whether it causes hurt, but a life without the light-hearted would be a sad place indeed.

My one fear in this corner of Scotland is that along with our Doric dialect, we are in danger of losing this special humour which we have treasured for generations as our very own characteristic. Being smacked across the fingers or made to stand out in class after lapsing into our native tongue has all but disappeared. Instead our educationalists are alive to the possibility that we might lose our heritage; the young find themselves encouraged to voice their natural tongue and thankfully are no longer vilified.

Life keeps moving on. Tried and tested medical treatments are discarded as old fashioned. School children are given a voice in how to run their schools. Standing back to allow ladies access before gentlemen is now seen by many women as sexist. Shaking hands has given way to pecks on the cheek or a male hug. Marriage is beginning to look old fashioned, while many young women appear to be the predators now instead of the men. Happily no one has so far banned us from laughing at ourselves as well as others, so there may yet be hope for our future.

BELIEFS, PREJUDICES AND OPINIONS

"FEW PEOPLE ARE CAPABLE OF EXPRESSING
WITH EQUANIMITY OPINIONS WHICH DIFFER
FROM THE PREJUDICES OF THEIR
SOCIAL ENVIRONMENT"

ALBERT EINSTEIN

Having pontificated across a broad spectrum of life, I have probably left some readers wondering exactly what I stand for, or believe in, so ready am I to propound some of the negatives in our behaviour. I feel it therefore incumbent on me to state clearly my stance in the arena of living, although I realise that this may incur further debate.

A belief should be distinguished from an opinion, although this is at times very difficult. I am persuaded as to the truthfulness of a belief, whereas when I have judged something is true, while accepting that I may be wrong, that is an opinion.

I believe that we are here on earth with one, and only one reason, and that is to procreate and maintain the species of homo sapiens. We are no different from every other living organism in battling to achieve this end. Our society has comfortably closed its eyes to such a base concept and focuses instead on the really important things in life. Education, employment, wealth, happiness and having children for the love of it, rather than thoughts of continuing the breed, conveniently ignore the reality. Just as we accept life and death, pondering on why we are here brings no joy or satisfaction, so the human mind has learnt sensibly to ignore it.

At a religious level I have no problem with either the Old or New Testaments in that they were the writings of that era, with only a rudimentary understanding of the world and appeared a reasonable recording for the times. While recognising that the King James I Bible of 1611 is a wonderful literary production and that it amended previous records to be more readily understood and made relevant to the Church of England, for me it is simply a historical work. Many of us, however, still base our understanding of life on these outdated concepts; like seeing the crystal set of a hundred years ago as the ultimate in radio communications and failing to move on.

It is disappointing that even after all these thousands of years we retain so many elements in our characters that demean us. Greed, jealousy, dishonesty, unreliability, anger, belligerence and prejudice all seem as dominant in our personalities as in Roman times and countless thousands of years before that. It is puzzling, as we become ever more sophisticated in appreciation of the world around us and all its wonders, that evolution does not begin to phase out some of our nastier failings. Perhaps I am just being impatient and this is all due to come about in another million years.

I do believe, despite all his faults and weaknesses, in the basic goodness of man. True, on many occasions this requires a lot of blind faith, but treated with understanding and consideration, man is inherently decent and caring. The horrible excesses of which he is capable often lie at the door of suspect leadership. The inherent tendency of the majority to follow has led to inhumane acts such as Hitler's extermination of the Jews, or the continuing senseless massacre of African tribes. Man is easily led and the cunning can contort evidence so obliquely that the majority fall for it every time.

The origin of life is much harder to define and here I have no belief, just an opinion. The answer seems to lie between a primitive life form being present on earth from its origins in space, or some chemical synthesis that occurred in the evolving conditions that came to exist millions of years ago. This, I am certain, will be solved within the next fifty years.

Yet another belief, which is really an opinion, is my attitude to the young. I am a firm believer in bringing up children to experience the rigours of life, away from the cushioned existence so many lead, especially in front of a TV or computer screen. Stretching them both physically as well as mentally makes them appreciate life so much more fully. Getting them involved in regular sport and making them walk or cycle instead of being carted around everywhere in motor transport, is so beneficial to their health. I applaud any initiative to promote this, such as the Duke of Edinburgh scheme.

Health and safety regulations stop many organisations from providing initiatives to toughen up our young, doing them a grave disservice. Yes, hazards can occur, but wrapping a generation in cotton wool is short sighted, both for their experience and for their future well-being. Wars are despicable, but they have some positive features in that the combatants begin to truly appreciate life, and gain immeasurably from the sharing of hardships and the companionship and trust in others; something most of our present generation have never been exposed to.

So we come to my prejudices, which I have tried valiantly over the years to eradicate without much success. I do not believe that massive tracts of our small island should ever be in the hands of the few, especially of foreigners. I accept that good landowners through the ages have brought work and a degree of prosperity to the local people. As with the Scottish Clearances, however, when the choice is between selfish self interest and the interests of the poor, there is only ever one loser.

"Are you a generous tipper?" seems a favourite media interview question, with the implication that it shows generosity to poorer mortals. My father through the 1930s more than doubled his annual salary through tips, so my abomination of the practice may appear rather incongruous. For me the tip identifies master and servant, though some may be quite happy with the arrangement. However it is the use of the *pourboire* on a commercial basis that undermines so much in society. Used by the hotel and restaurant trades as well as tourism, especially in the USA, to keep running costs low, many depend on the generosity of the clientele to keep their staff happy and reasonably recompensed.

Getting the best table in a West End restaurant may be down to celebrity, but also a heavy expected tip which is good for the maître d'hôtel, but I much prefer to be welcomed as a pleasant guest than fussed deceitfully at the cost of the outstretched hand. What was once a genuine thankyou has become not only expected but demanded, as I have experienced more than once in America. I can hear the scoffers say that this is just the way of the world, but travel to the Antipodes and try tipping the average Aussie. He will soon tell you he is no man's serf so don't try treating him like one. An honest approach that tells you immediately that he is just treating you as he would have you treat him.

I like to feel I have no racial prejudice and having a mixture of French and English blood, I am no one to criticise. However, the feeling of kinship with your fellow man starts on your doorstep and as you travel further there can be a lessening of that bond. The local Doric dialect has me feeling totally at home, but in the early days the accents from further south felt alien, while even the Glasgow twang was foreign to me and liable to arouse my suspicions. World travel has almost eliminated those early feelings, but I am still a great believer that incomers should blend with the locals and not brazenly try to take over or impose their values.

With Islam rearing its head across the world, with some adherents becoming ever more militant, I have to accept that I am prejudiced against the wearing of the burka. I feel that this is totally against our culture and is an artificial barrier in a free society. It is liable to be frightening to other citizens and in a nation worried about terrorism is a real or imagined threat to our security. The wearer may say that the burka is an integral part of her belief, but she is selfishly ignoring the rights and anxieties of the indigenous population. I believe the French are correct in banning it in public and the sooner this is tackled in this country the better, before it becomes a cult symbol with ever more adherents.

In the same vein, I have strong feelings about faith schools as a divisive element in society, especially in areas such as Glasgow, where religious intolerance has thrived for far too long. Church schools with mixed intakes and which provide an excellent education without forcing pupils to bow down before religious doctrine are acceptable, but those veering towards blinkered creationism or subtly promoting religious intolerance should be heavily supervised or ideally closed down.

Under the surface I also have to fight my prejudice over irritation with parenting, where young children are exhibiting far more than just puppy fat. To sit in a restaurant and watch obese young people gorging on hamburgers and pizzas, while their parents either sit idly by, or gorge themselves in a similar manner, makes me as a doctor totally despondent. I am very conscious of my disturbing level of prejudice over gross disfiguring obesity, while the mobile phone at the ear of every other passer-by has me wondering what will be the next innovation to grab this generation by the throat.

I tend to be suspicious, even slightly prejudiced, against past glamorous heroes, although I have huge appreciation of the efforts of others. Coming from the generation that lived through that gorgeous summer of 1940, the clear blue skies were memorable for the Spitfire and Hurricane pilots who gave their lives to keep Hitler at bay. Those memories make me thankful for such warriors, but I realise that called to do our duty, we would have responded in similar fashion, so hero worship is unnecessary. Too many heroes of the past have turned out to be of doubtful quality, so it is wise never to set people on a pedestal, as they almost invariably come a cropper.

The recent celebrity culture of making heroes out of entertainers, whom I see as totally unworthy, makes me dismissive of my fellow man. With the majority of us as followers, many are only too delighted to find heroes in all walks of life, but at times this borders on the inane and is not only found among the uneducated. Popular television programmes often plumb the depths of demeaning entertainment, which panders to some of the unsavoury bits of our nature and here I do get very prejudiced. I well recognise my blanket judgement is unfair, but I do dissipate some of my irritation by being able to express it.

Crafty politicians really get under my skin with such quotes as "trust the people". Anyone thinking that you can trust such an amorphous group, with a multiplicity of attitudes, often associated with ignorance and prejudice, and able to change direction overnight is either totally stupid or extremely devious.

On the world scene I am truly prejudiced against the state of Israel, or perhaps disappointed is a better term. Not that it acts much worse than many other emerging violent nations, but that its people have seen fit to learn nothing from their own past. A gifted and influential tribe, but suppressed and humiliated for generations, having their own homeland was the opportunity to show the rest of the world, with a Mandela insight, that some men can rise above the ills of narrow self interest and show the rest of us the way.

Instead with their various fanatical factions they are gradually squeezing the Palestinians into ever smaller enclaves with overwhelming brute force. Instead of becoming more sensitive to the suffering of others, their Nazi and Russian pogrom experiences appear to have made them totally impervious to unfairness and bullying. A truly sad outcome, but we should have been warned when they initially acted like any other terrorist organisation themselves against the British, costing many innocent service lives just trying to do their duty for peace in the region.

I am very conscious that throughout these chapters there is an underlying apparent bias against America. It is true I am highly critical of some aspects of its life style; at times there is evidence of US insensitivity and frankly ignorance in much of its foreign policy. Perhaps predominant nations throughout the ages all tended to ride rough shod over the feelings and interests of lesser nations, with the British Empire being no exception. However, with universal media coverage bringing the world into everyone's living-room, there is the impression that Americans remain essentially only interested in their own back yard, when not chasing terrorists or promoting themselves as the ultimate religious adherents. Delightful people, but very much geared to success, prosperity, glitz and their very own gun laws, while convinced they belong to God's own country. A nation of stark contrasts highlighted by that beacon of American freedom, the magnificent White House – built by slaves.

Pausing to recall Einstein's opening quote to this chapter I am aware I have just committed the cardinal sin he refers to. Such armchair criticism of a mighty nation is small minded and although partially true, ignores the huge benefits the US has brought to the world. So easy to highlight the faults and ignore the successes; the broad picture is so much more subtle and I should temper my views and accept that it will be the historians of the future who will properly assess the place of the USA in the history of the world.

No, my nagging prejudice regarding the US should be levelled at our own politicians who demean the nation by stressing a 'special relationship', reminding me of those prepared to curry favour with the playground bully in my far off schooldays.

One final prejudice remains regarding the materialism of modern life. Out in the private sector, our leaders of industry, and particularly the financial world, have got used to receiving massive salaries and bonuses of multiple millions a year. Now, in the public sector we are brainwashed to believe that to get the best we also have to pay enormous salaries to attract the talented. What on earth does any man or woman need so much money for and what does this tell us about the shallowness of life?

If people only work to accumulate money and possessions, we have reached the nadir of human civilisation. Yes, some like Bill Gates bequeath their wealth to good causes, but we require a gale of wind throughout the world to make the accumulation of obscene wealth a sign of man's decadence, not his ultimate success.

Moving on then to opinions, the individual in society has very little opportunity or power to make much difference at either local or national level. The ballot box gives some semblance of choice, but so diluted that many feel it a worthless right. Similarly the voting rights of small shareholders are relatively worthless as the institutions with their large holdings have all the clout. Democracy is so often a charade, manipulated by those with vested interests to baffle and confound the little man in the street. Have I an opinion how to improve it? No.

Not an opinion, but a pondering. If leaders and followers had been instructed to have a greater understanding of themselves could such disasters as Hitler's rise to power been averted? Thousands and thousands of disciplined goose-stepping German troops and now North Koreans are on parade, appearing to have had their minds anaesthetised; could all of this have been halted by introducing them to insight? Radicalisation of Muslim youth in the UK is an increasing problem, while the US Christian right continues to produce extremists. Could these foot soldiers have been saved from being putty in the hands of fanatical leaders and teachers, if from an early age they had been given more insight? If they were taught to recognise why they were doing things, and to think more for themselves, then surely we could begin to live in a more sensible and logical world.

True, too much introspection could have us rooted to the spot in case we only appeared to be following our predestined responses. Football fans would stay at home and mope, while race goers would deny their interest in case someone put them in the Royal Ascot basket. Certainly there is so much more to life than serious contemplation and navel gazing. However, in world affairs a little more insight and honest understanding would not come amiss among our leaders and their henchmen.

While recognised by psychologists as a dangerous field for some, educational courses to define who you are in this life can be very rewarding. Unhappily, this can undermine some individuals' perception of themselves. I have experienced mature doctors reduced to tears and seen one or two change direction in careers and lifestyle after such exposure.

The other memorable outcome was that some doctors were unable to conceive the purpose of the exercise and came away scornfully dismissive of the experience. This inability to comprehend appeared similar to colour blindness, but was interesting in the case of GPs, when it is taken for granted they are reasonably proficient in counselling patients for mental problems, yet incapable of understanding themselves.

Inheriting a relatively uncommon gene making me neither leader nor ready follower gives me a rather oblique slant on life. From my fly on the wall view, I can feel rather detached from many leaders and followers, but does it allow me any greater insight into the intricacies of our society? Does this make my beliefs, prejudices and opinions any more pertinent than that of my fellow man? My need to desert my wall perch all too readily to get involved in events shows sadly that I am not after all an impartial observer, but proves my equal fallibility with those on whom I would be so tempted to sit in judgement.

TIME TO PONDER

**"HEALTH IS THE GREATEST POSSESSION,
CONTENTMENT IS THE GREATEST TREASURE.
CONFIDENCE IS THE GREATEST FRIEND.
NON-BEING IS THE GREATEST JOY"**

LAO TZU
Chinese Taoist Philosopher

Are you likely to be one of those in St Peter's Square, hanging on to the words of your beloved Pope? No, then you are preening yourself that you have a ticket for the Centre Court at Wimbledon, although you have never seriously held a tennis racket in your life. If young enough, you would rather be packed together like sardines among ecstatic revellers at the

Glastonbury Festival. Wherever you are in this sort of setting you are happy to be in close proximity to your fellow man, which tells me that I shall probably not be rubbing shoulders with you.

For me, my fellow man is best in a one-to-one setting – half a dozen or more around me and the world is crowding in. Perhaps it is indicative of the only child upbringing and the days of solitary, but happy existence. Time to contemplate has always been a top priority and I get no pleasure from being surrounded by hordes of people. I admire those who take to the streets in fury, as at the time of the Iraq conflict and Tony Blair's gross error of judgement, but I would rather sit and write a letter to *The Times*, in the knowledge that it would never be published. In some peculiar fashion I would feel I had done my duty without getting caught up in a noisy demonstration among a bunch of strangers. Totally foolish and the lazy man's attitude and I do feel ashamed, but console myself that one more on the streets would make no difference.

Standing back from the crowd and not getting caught up in the minutiae of social living can be a strength, but also a weakness. Expressing thoughts that are at variance with the majority can give a sense of individuality, but can also make you seem an outsider and a renegade to those around you. Being known as the one who is always at odds with many popular aspects of life is not easy and at times I just acquiesce and drift along.

Does my lack of enthusiasm for the theatre, concerts, opera and exhibitions come from lack of intellect, disinterest or coming from a background where such sophisticated pastimes were above my ceiling? Probably the answer is some of each as I look back with regret to never persevering to play a musical instrument or being trained to sing. Somewhere in my soul there is still a longing to take up so many of these interests, but somehow life has passed them by. Also my distaste for built up areas makes visiting the cities of the world more often a chore than a pleasure, while the wild wide open spaces of the world are something I cherish and yearn for in old age.

Although I purport to have no heroes, I do at times feel some envy for the abilities of others. Many say that to have been a relatively successful doctor and written books in my retirement should have been success enough, but it is a human failing to think that so much more could and should have been achieved. Looking back in my life I can see where the crossroads have occurred and where another route could have led to a totally different outcome, but then hindsight is a pointless exercise. I have no regrets and well recognise that I have been extremely lucky and should now count my blessings. However, ploughing a virgin furrow in life from modest beginnings has none of the benefits of those children brought up and given purpose and direction from a middle-class, educated background. Something I fully appreciated in setting my own children on the path to achievement and security.

Themes throughout this book look at emotional issues like homosexuality, rape and paedophilia with the object of drawing attention to the contrarian view that it is not as clear-cut and dried as public opinion would like to suggest. The tendency of ordinary people to react like a lynch mob is also considered, while some of our other freedoms appear under threat from too much bureaucracy.

An area which may raise some negative comment is the chapter when I attempt to pigeon-hole individuals on their personality traits. This is something I have been intrigued with over the last forty years and which I believe has still to be fully recognised by the ordinary person. One reason is that like talking about intelligence there are winners and losers. It seems that so sensitive have we become that anything which appears to separate goats from sheep or horses from donkeys has to be swept out of sight. That the majority of people can be projected as lemmings following the latest trend or fad raises hackles all round, but the unfortunate truth is that evolution has predestined our roles in life.

Personality is a subject that throughout my career in the medical profession was studiously ignored, sending out the message it was so liable to traumatise some individuals that we should leave it alone, like turning our backs on an unexploded bomb. The almost unbelievable control of the German nation by Hitler is still largely overlooked by the public media. Yet the ability of one man to mesmerise a highly civilised and cultured nation in the way he did, suggests a messianic ability, not unlike that of Jesus of Nazareth. This is a field of thought which so far has scarcely touched the average citizen, yet is the very same influence that can fill a stadium to see the Pope.

I have failed to address many areas on which readers would have expected some comment. For someone as old as me, the sanctity of marriage should have arisen. I have always believed marriage is an extremely difficult union, with men in particular not programmed to have only one mate. It says a great deal for our past discipline and adhering to convention to have kept it going for so long, but for all its difficulties I believe it provides the greatest benefits in bringing up children. Over the past decades the acceptance of partnership without any formal responsibility does not strike me as a move in the right direction. However, it is perhaps more honest than marriages lasting a few months or years making the whole set-up a total farce. A £20,000 to £50,000 posh wedding and then only a token marriage is for me the sign of a spoilt and shallow generation, which makes me very sad and disillusioned.

Knowing the cost of everything and the value of nothing is a popular saying, highly relevant in these times. I sense that the middle and upper classes earn far too much money for their own good. In my practice I found some of the happiest and most contented of our patients often had the least. To have just enough and a little to put past for a rainy day seemed so satisfying for them, whereas our oil executives with everything provided had some of the most dissatisfied of wives.

Better to travel than to arrive is an old proverb not practised by many today, with children and adults alike indulging their wishes on a whim. My greatest treasures in life are those which I have wished for and achieved only after much tedious endeavour.

There seems to be a soullessness about society due to a mixture of a generation on an aimless path in life, bored and yet with enough money to go searching for cheap pleasures. An inane celebrity culture fuelled by shrewd businessmen soon parts the younger generation from its money. In the past the working class battled to make ends meet, but now in a far wealthier world we have been unable to provide the mass of mankind in this country with anything more meaningful to strive for other than money, possessions and pleasure. The real disappointment for me however is to be found not down among the poor but in the top echelons where the scramble for more and more filthy lucre originates. Our leaders in all walks of life at this level continue to show nothing but avarice, never appearing to have enough, so it is little wonder that those of lesser stature learn no more worthwhile values.

An area I have failed to tackle in the broad sweep of life and of huge relevance in our world today is the abuse of alcohol and the increasing use of mood enhancing drugs. Like so many other observers I do not possess any magic bullet and this is why I have not focussed more fully on it. The Scottish culture of not being a real man if you can't take a drink is very difficult to eradicate, especially in certain sections of society. As a doctor I am so aware of the inherited hazards that alcohol and drugs present and the lack of insight into such problems by those around them. The availability of cheap potent alcohol for our young to sample is certainly an area for a careful rethink. Our copycat culture affects none more so than children, with their need for branded products and latest electronic equipment, so alcohol abuse is a constant concern if it rates highly in their peer group. Pricing it partially out of their reach is one method but it really requires society, especially adolescent society, to begin to recognise drunkenness as crude and degrading behaviour. Unfortunately, escape from the drudgery of apparently hopeless lives in an alcoholic or drugged haze is a difficult problem to counter.

Having had no exposure to the drug culture, it is difficult for me to form a worthwhile opinion. However there does seem a King Canute type of mindset to the problem which will never win. Just as prohibition in America drove alcohol underground to the benefit of the dishonest and made vast fortunes for the few, so it appears that society is now riddled with suppliers, traders and addicts caught up in an ever-widening profitable business. Hard as the decision must be, the only way to disrupt this cancer is by legalising drugs and accepting that there may be consequences for the minority. Ready access under control conditions would puncture the trade and then allow us to focus all our efforts on rehabilitation, education and working to stigmatise the habit. All so easy to write about, but to put it into action will be a real challenge for the future.

Throughout the ages societies have varied in their treatment of the so-called wrongdoers. Throwing them to the lions, firing them out of canons, putting them in the stocks or just decapitating them, man has shown little mercy. Sent to Australia for stealing a loaf of bread has us still teasing the Aussie about his convict ancestry.

At the present time we simply lock ever more into our expanding prison system on the basis that if they are out of sight they can't do us harm. The fact that re-offending after prison is unacceptably high and that many are only further criminalised by their prison experience seems all too much for our administrators to counter. For the budding and persistent criminal a prison sentence is a badge of honour – scarcely the desired effect – while for those caught up in more minor offences the legal process is almost enough of a disgrace without locking them up. Prison must be there for the dangerous and the hardened criminals, but for a large proportion of others more imaginative penalties must be developed. Loss of privileges in their normal life styles could be severe deterrents, such as removing their freedom of movement, or banning them from driving while having a well structured community service taskforce requiring an eight hour stint so many times a week. It is so obvious that the present is a failed system and needs a radical rethink.

When contemplating this problem I well remember that Johnny Cash song live from San Quentin prison and particularly the lyrics. "San Quentin you cut me and scarred me through and through. What good do you think you do? Do you think I'll be different when you're through?" These emotional lyrics somehow give a true sense of the hopelessness of dealing with our misfits and trespassers by simply locking them away and forgetting them. The question of revenge and making culprits suffer for their offences is something which plays a large part in many people's attitudes and has held back sensible reform. The major need is to reduce the number turning to crime in the first instance, but this also appears beyond the wit of society to tackle with bleak, threatening estates ensuring a steady pool of the disenfranchised.

The approach by Kenneth Clarke in the Coalition Government to send fewer offenders to prison showed a welcome rethink. However without a massive rehabilitation, educational and employment programme put in place first of all, it has the appearance of a short term initiative not backed up by the necessary funding, organisation or general agreement among parliamentarians, never mind the general public.

Out of the blue the vicious riots and looting of August 2011 took those of us living in our sleepy leafy suburbs totally by surprise. Suddenly we realised that deep down there among our most deprived were elements of fury, violence and sheer criminality that defied the image we treasured of us as a modern civilised democracy propounding its values across the world. A breakdown of the tribal family structure and of its strengths across all society appears now as a root cause. There has been gang culture among young men throughout generations, but it now appears to have displaced the family in importance among the most deprived. Here we also come to that unspoken reality that ignorance, stupidity and unthinking subservience play a huge part in this field, where sweet reason will always struggle to be understood. For those of us termed wishy-washy liberals, in attempting to treat all members of society fairly, the latest outbreak of violence and looting firmly demonstrates that only the iron fist in the velvet glove is viable for the way ahead.

There are areas which take little change of direction to offer some hope for the future. Discipline has become a tainted word over the past decades, nowhere more evident than in our schools. In my day I was liable to get a second dressing down at home after the strap at school, whereas many parents now appear to see any form of school discipline as victimisation. Giving back authority to teachers while keeping parents fully informed of the ethos of the school does not seem to be a backward step, as long as the harshness of some teachers in the past is eliminated.

I look on my National Service with a sense of giving something back to the nation whereas all that had gone before was about self interest. I well understand the difficulties in this field for the present generation, but still believe it has benefits far beyond simply giving up say two years of your life in what may seem a diversion from careers and work, especially for those more interested in non-employment. Such service could offer a wide choice ranging from the military to humanitarian, cultural or public service, but with the underlying object of civilising, disciplining and broadening outlooks which should pay huge dividends for the future of the young. Simply slotting such service into the end of formal school education at age sixteen to eighteen for all could soon be accepted as the norm, but of course has huge financial and organisational obstacles. Such momentous decisions to instigate are where true, insightful leadership is required and from past evidence has little hope of realisation.

Viewing the crime and prison scenes on TV from America does make one pause and wonder whether we moderates are simply whistling in the wind to think that common sense and a humane approach will ever be able to combat the brutalisation of life as demonstrated by criminals and the authorities alike in the USA.

The part played by our media in the general deterioration of standards and common decency in society can not be over emphasised. From the brain washing, as exemplified by the efforts of the Murdoch empire, through other unbalanced and crude TV and press coverage to the advertising world, life is trivialised. A wonderland of material possessions for young and old alike assails the average brain, separating us by a million miles from those in poverty across the world that we quietly ignore.

Pondering the poor and dispossessed has many facets, but one in particular shows the limits of both our attention span and ability to put ourselves into other people's situations. The enemy's casualties of war, including their civilians, are accepted as of little moment, while even one death on our side is a tragedy. It is the dismissive way that the innocent mean so little to particularly the Americans that really shocks. Increasingly the American message "Land of the free" becomes ever more tarnished with its attitude of "might and right" resonating unfeelingly around the world.

Time to ponder has a double meaning, just as in our cryptic crosswords. To ponder about time is a subject surely deserving of more than a few lines. Time varies throughout our lives — crawling through a school week to disappear in a cloud of dust over a week-end. Never ending when tedium is around, but escaping us all too quickly in enjoyment. The holiday of a lifetime seems always months away, but has come and gone in a haze of memories, leaving us somewhat unfulfilled. The years of childhood seemed to go on for ever – summer holidays with the sun shining every day until that final week-end when reality reminds us that this school year heralds that new teacher – the feared school tartar.

Similarly throughout life, time was ever a changing experience. Apprehensive one minute, enthralled the next, but often leaving me drained and dejected but always looking back and wondering where it had all gone. Never able to conquer the pace; it dragged when a minute seemed a lifetime, but an evening in love was past in the blink of an eye. Then there are the occasions when time seems to stop and we are isolated in eternity. Not that I can get my friends to sense this, but when sitting waiting for the traffic lights to change, time seems suspended and I wonder if the world has paused for a breather, just for an instant.

Now retired for twenty years, I cannot comprehend how that time has passed. Being the happiest and most carefree years of my life, I take it that this is one reason for its apparent brevity. There seems little doubt that with advancing years the brain's appreciation of time diminishes and so hours flash past at an ever-increasing pace. As I plough into my eighties I try on occasions to slow this onward rush by just sitting idly doing nothing, counting minutes instead of hours, but all to no avail with next week already upon me.

Occasionally I listen to the middle-aged decrying the benefits of old age, for instance in being able to play golf every waking hour while they are confined to only weekends. They would happily see the back of us or make us pay extra for the privilege of so much leisure, but they show a frightening lack of insight into time. When I tell them they will be old tomorrow, they perceive me as senile, but unhappily they will wake up all too soon to find they are the ones being reviled by their juniors. Meanwhile my shooting days no longer has the shoot leader

Malcolm shouting at me for missing yet again, but now he hails my every success with whoops of enthusiasm and not a little amazement. Yes, time is no one's servant and for me throughout my life has been friend and foe in almost equal measure.

The other unknown about time has been dutifully ignored throughout this book, as I shall not be around to view it. Much passion and little light is generated by the arguments regarding global warming and when this shall come to pass. I have little doubt that the increasing turbulence in our weather is related to this phenomenon. Whether this will result in a steady exodus north for populations when drought and heat become all too much is a frightening thought, but thankfully for most of us, this is a problem for another generation.

Time has removed the safe haven of my childhood while the strong independence of my working life is now behind me. My children no longer defer to me, but tend to treat me with slight amusement and I find looking around that my cosy brotherhood of contemporaries has thinned out alarmingly. While I am writing this book my dear wife gradually succumbs to the dreaded cancer and slips away peacefully on the 22nd of March 2011 to leave behind a horrible void which months later has still the feeling of unreality.

Now when those around me talk of 20 years hence, I sadly realise they are talking about their lives not mine. There is no place for self pity, as we have done our duty as we saw it and the children and grandchildren are out there to continue our genetic line. Most of us still have a long way to go to understanding ourselves, while the ability of the human brain has still huge potential for a great leap forward when science begins to unravel its intricacies. The future can only be seen through a thick haze at present, but as long as our leaders keep their finger off the self destruct nuclear button, our great-great-grandchildren may well look back on us as a very primitive generation.

These ponderings, first as an only child with so much time on my hands and now in retirement, have given me hours of pleasure and continue to keep me company so I never need to feel alone. As for time itself, it can be a great companion or a wicked enemy, but right now I am not going to insult it any further just in case it has evil thoughts of calling time on yet another frail mortal.

This little book has been fun to write as it embodies so many of the bees in my bonnet and also the problems that have whirled about in my brain over decades. The whole tenor of the book may feel very serious, but throughout life I have always attempted to keep things in proportion, with a laugh and a bit of banter to leaven serious argument.

I accept that many will not only disagree, but possibly be upset with some of my ideas. Some indeed may dismiss much as unworthy of their consideration. However the great freedom in our nation is to hold different views from one another, this being the life blood for discussion. Tangential and controversial thinking is meant to be uncomfortable and irritating, but is a necessary perquisite for the broadening of minds and hopefully moving forward man's mission to improve the world around us.

After all, kicking sleeping dogs was never meant to be a hazard-free venture.

The Taoist philosopher Lao Tzu heads this chapter so let him finish with an explanation of Non-being is the greatest joy. In all things you do it is not what you do – the being – that is of most importance. It is the guiding principle and significance of what you do – the non-being – which should concern you most. Oh to be a philosopher!

FINALE

"I NEVER SUBMITTED THE WHOLE SYSTEM OF
MY OPINIONS TO THE CREED OF ANY PARTY OF
MEN WHATEVER, IN RELIGION, IN
PHILOSOPHY, IN POLITICS OR IN ANYTHING
ELSE, WHERE I WAS CAPABLE OF THINKING FOR
MYSELF. SUCH AN ADDICTION IS THE LAST
DEGRADATION OF A FREE AND MORAL AGENT.
IF I COULD NOT GO TO HEAVEN BUT WITH A
PARTY, I WOULD NOT GO THERE AT ALL."

THOMAS JEFFERSON (1743-1824)
President - United States of America

Jefferson's telling quote is something that resonates very
powerfully with my own thoughts. I have to admit quite

frankly that I have never come close to his ideals, but its message has been my guiding light throughout the decades.

Jefferson must have been a very determined and driven man to achieve such strengths at a time when the world seemed a much smaller place and where, for instance, religious conformity would have been expected even from a United States leader.

I envy those who have the ability to stick to their principles through thick and thin. Very few of us ever come near to achieving this and throughout my career I could never be sure if fronting up opposition to some proposal or party was either wise or worthwhile.

At school I quickly learnt that you could land yourself as the fall guy if expressing a point of view to authority which all had agreed, until challenged, when your brave henchmen were nowhere to be found. Similarly at University it was prudent never to jeopardise your future by being fingered as a rebel. Very much like physical courage, mental courage is something we all have in differing proportions. Some quiet inoffensive people turn out as heroes, whereas extrovert bully boys have feet of clay. I rate myself as fairly average, except that I do get quite upset when no one stands up for the under privileged or when unfairness goes blatantly unchallenged.

In General Practice I would have been rated a rebel against the all powerful elders who dictated our lives. It was not a role I fancied, but such was the level of dominance accepted by my colleagues that I just could not look myself in the face if I did not rouse myself to take a stand. Branded as a troublemaker, it took years of genuine involvement to improve my standing until gradually my credibility was recognised. Not a happy experience, as many in my peer group showed their true colours, only joining the fight when the tide had turned. It is a very sad reflection on human nature that so many depend on the few to do the fighting, but like jackals are only too happy to join in once victory is secured.

It would be unfair to brand all compliant people as weak, as there were many decent, honourable doctors in my time that diligently went about their profession, but did not wish to get involved in the unpleasantness of challenging the status quo. A quiet life of helping the sick is all they sought and I have no problem with such attitudes, but it is a poor nation that can not find a few minor Jeffersons to battle unfairness and bureaucracy. The crowning glory in my late career was when some of my younger colleagues fingered me as the establishment figure in the district, so as with the passing of time, nothing stands still.

Jefferson talks about thinking for oneself, but here again far too many of us, despite our education, remain embedded in outdated attitudes and subservient ways. Nowhere is this more evident than when involved in political canvassing and finding the responses from the average citizen. "Always been a blue blood Tory" or "always vote Labour as the party of the people", were frequent responses, which made you despair of the right to vote. Democracy is a wonderful concept, but like one of my favourite quotes that, "youth is wasted on the young", far too many scarcely think independently. Political parties are never static and the intelligent should shrewdly assess their policies, if only to decide which suits their own particular interests. Balanced against this of course are those who change sides at the first sign of tough measures making governing a country a nightmare. In many ways I believe in a paternalistic dictatorship, but only if the dictator was a Mandela-like figure.

Looking back, I can resurrect memories when I have totally failed to live up to my own standards and have always regretted them. Not always standing up to some bullies in my very young days in the playground, when weaker chums were being given a hard life, is something I regret. Fear of physical violence was probably at the root of this, just as I failed to intervene in an assault on a couple by a gang of youths in Dundee. Failing to face up to staff in an old folks home, who were treating patients with no respect, has also lived on with me through the years. Unhappy that I could make life worse all round if I intervened was no excuse; it showed poor judgement and a fear of upsetting authority.

Similarly, in a packed hotel foyer in London returning home from holiday, witnessing the victimisation of an Indian lady is also very embarrassing. The lady, pleading for help as her flight had been cancelled and her luggage was missing, was being loudly abused by an Englishman behind her telling her she should get out of our way. The likes of her should stay at home as we didn't want her sort of foreigner in our country. Over thirty of us stood idly by as she looked hopefully at us for some support, yet not one intervened, with the lady now in floods of tears at this outrage. I restrained the urge to speak up wondering who was braver than me, but there was no one and I had failed the test of decency – sad for me but doubly sad for us as a caring nation.

Why do I highlight such inadequacies? It is because none of us can really lecture one another as I feel certain we have all failed to live up to our own standards sometime in our lives. I could highlight many more of my failures, but I have at least tried to learn lessons so that faced with similar problems, although not now involving violence, I would make a far better stab at solving them. Yes, we are all just fallible human beings, but it does no harm to read again Jefferson's words and at least try to apply a few such gems into the odd strand of our lives.

So can I draw any inferences from the research that has gone into the preceding chapters? Certainly as I have progressed from our primitive beginnings, through the age of religions up to the present day, with the world having seen the fall of fascism and communism, there does seems an uncanny resemblance between so many of these apparently unrelated episodes.

Only by standing back can I discern through history that although the events are all different, man's input and reaction to them has almost been unvarying. Leaders leading and followers blindly following is the story across the world throughout the ages. Remembering one major ingredient of leadership as detailed in What Are You – Cat or Dog? is "suspension of critical thinking" and this seems applicable to nearly every major event and mass response from Jesus Christ to Adolf Hitler.

One of my great regrets in a long life is now to doubt any so-called facts without uncontroversial evidence. Whether at a local level or up to the affairs of state, man has an unenviable reputation of twisting the truth to suit his needs. Whether my attitude is termed scepticism or cynicism, there is little doubt that it is far better to doubt something and have it proved correct than take an optimistic attitude towards your fellow man and be totally hoodwinked. The Institute of Advanced Motorists teaches that nothing must ever be taken for granted, even down to believing that drivers indicating left won't suddenly turn right. This is a lesson which is valuable out into the wider world.

The Iraq war has been such an example and only now are we uncovering the truth behind an apparently duplicitous Tony Blair and his actions. The power of the State with its propaganda machine backed up by a blinkered media sold the British public a totally distorted picture, causing hundreds of thousands of dead including our own citizens. The tragedy was far greater than one man, however, in just the same way as the Harold Shipman murders went far beyond one guilty person.

The whole structure of the state failed over Iraq: the Cabinet failed, Parliament failed, the Foreign Office failed, the media failed, the legal system failed while the Chiefs of Staff failed their own men by taking them into a conflict they were unprepared for. Many of us also failed as we dismissed the UN evidence and blindly followed leaders distorting the truth, although a wonderful rally of a million people in London showed the world some really cared. In future, however, combine another ignorant Bush and a lackey Blair and will we have learnt any lessons at all? From the evidence through the ages the answer is not one iota.

Man's brain unravels the most intricate problems, develops wonders in the world and even puts a man on the moon, but human behaviour has scarcely altered from the days of Moses. Some may point out that Britain by progressively becoming a secular state is showing for once an independence of thought at last and moving away from mysticism. True, the young and not so young appear to have turned their backs on their religion, but I believe this is not from any deep progressive thought, but more due to the fact that religion is at present simply unfashionable. There is no peer pressure to show faith, no drawback to their jobs to say they don't believe and who would want to give up their Sundays to go to church?

The statistics comparing the UK to the US regarding religion and how it is perceived is like looking at extreme opposites. Shaking our heads in sadness for those simple minded Americans swallowing all this religious mysticism should be tempered with some insight. Given a sudden revivalist movement in the UK with a charismatic leader, we could soon find millions of adherents flocking to hear the message. Human behaviour has never changed in the past, so just as in the Weimar Republic, Germans turned their back on common sense and invested in the grandiose schemes of a dictator, so we should be very careful in not getting too superior.

The human mind has been at the core of this book with religion being used as one of the main subjects to demonstrate, not only its frailties, but also some of its strengths. Other areas have also been called in to further examine how we function in society and how we, mostly unconsciously, adapt to our surroundings and fellow human beings. The fact that only a small percentage of the population are aware of the part they are playing on this stage of life is quite remarkable in this day and age. Perhaps our educationalists are very aware of the inherent dangers of too much concentrated insight into what we do and why we do it, so are perfectly correct in leaving those sleeping dogs undisturbed.

There is also little doubt that close to home and right out across the world there is a significant minority of people who function at a totally different level from the average citizen. Insightful, intelligent and devious they pull the strings at all strata of society to further their aims unseen and unheralded. So much that occurs in our lives is not what it seems, but is governed by the few. However, for us as innocents it is perhaps best that this should remain largely unrecognised or we could become even more cynical as a nation.

Reaching conclusions on our own lives can never be truly unbiased, but there is so much learning from past generations which we continually fail to observe in our own day to day living. The strengths and weaknesses of man are unchanging, so predicting outcomes at personal, family, community, national and world levels is not rocket science. Our patterns of behaviour appear ageless as everything flows from Professor Dawkins perceptions as expounded in *The Selfish Gene*, first published in 1976. Dawkins maintains that genes can be thought of as having a 'selfish' desire for immortality through survival and reproduction. In fact he states "the predominant quality to be expected of a successful gene is ruthless selfishness". A basic concept many may still find difficult to acknowledge, but is the harsh truth of life as is well illustrated by the cuckoo's apparent cruelty in perpetuating her species at the expense of others.

For some of us this is an intriguing jungle to explore, but for the majority just getting on with life as it presents is far more practical. Is it too much to expect that for those with the intelligence and interest, we pause in life from time to time and perceive, much more closely, our own actions and hence with increased insight resolve to be better family members, friends and citizens in such an uncertain world?

IF YOU WANT HAPPINESS FOR AN HOUR,
TAKE A NAP;
IF YOU WANT HAPPINESS FOR A DAY,
GO FISHING;
IF YOU WANT HAPPINESS FOR A MONTH,
GET MARRIED;
IF YOU WANT HAPPINESS FOR A YEAR,
INHERIT A FORTUNE;
IF YOU WANT HAPPINESS FOR A LIFETIME,
HELP SOMEONE ELSE.

Chinese Proverb

Book References

Brown, D. (2003). *THE DA VINCI CODE.* Bantam Press

Dawkins, R. (1976). *THE SELFISH GENE.* Oxford University Press

Dawkins, R. (2006). *THE GOD DELUSION.* Bantam Press

Fouin, F.L.P. (2005). *THE EARLY LIFE AND TIMES OF A GLEN TANAR EXILE.* Librario Publishing

Fouin, F.L.P. (2009). *GLEN TANAR – Valley of Echoes and Hidden Treasures.* Leopard Press

Galileo, G. (1632). *DIALOGUE CONCERNING THE TWO CHIEF WORLD SYSTEMS*

Gordon, R. (1952). *DOCTOR IN THE HOUSE.* Penguin Books

Hamer, D. (2005). *THE GOD GENE: How Faith is Hard-wired into our Genes.* Anchor Books

KING JAMES BIBLE – begun 1604 completed 1611. Printed by Robert Baker

Mullins, C. (2009). *A VIEW FROM THE FOOTHILLS.* Profile Books

Odone, C. (2009). *WHAT WOMEN WANT – And How They can Get It.* Centre for Policy Studies

Weatherhead, Rev L.D. (1931) *THE MASTERY OF SEX.* Student Christian Movement, London